Warrior • 31

Union Infantryman
1861–65

John Langellier • Illustrated by John White

First published in Great Britain in 2001 by Osprey Publishing,
Midland House, West Way, Botley, Oxford OX2 0PH, UK
44-02 23rd St, Suite 219, Long Island City, NY 11101, USA
E-mail: info@ospreypublishing.com

Transferred to digital print on demand 2009

First published 2001
2nd impression 2005

Printed and bound by Cadmus Communications, USA

A CIP catalog record for this book is available from the British Library

ISBN: 978 1 84176 176 3

Editor: Nikolai Bogdanovic
Design: The Black Spot
Index by Alan Rutter
Originated by Grasmere Digital Imaging, Leeds, UK

Artist's Note

Readers may care to note that the original paintings from which the color plates in this book were prepared are available for private
sale. All reproduction copyright whatsoever is retained by the Publishers. All enquiries should be addressed to:

John White, 5107 C Monroe Road, Charlotte, NC 28205, United States of America

The Publishers regret that they can enter into no correspondence upon this matter.

Author's Note

Dedicated to Maj. Gen. Robert L.Drudik, USA (Ret), the epitome of an officer, a gentleman, and a combat infantryman.

Acknowledgments and Credits

The author wishes to thank Christopher Anderson, C. Paul Loane, Dr Michael J. McAfee (MM), Walt RedIng (WR), and Dr Vincent A.
Transano for their assistance, as well as staff members of the Gettysburg National Military Park (GNMP), U.S. Army Military History
Institute (USAMHI), Smithsonian Institution (SI), National Archives (NA) , and Library of Congress (LC). Numerals indicated after Library
of Congress images are negative identification numbers.

FOR A CATALOG OF ALL BOOKS PUBLISHED BY OSPREY
MILITARY AND AVIATION PLEASE CONTACT:

Osprey Direct, c/o Random House Distribution Center,
400 Hahn Road, Westminster, MD 21157
Email: uscustomerservice@ospreypublishing.com

Osprey Direct, The Book Service Ltd, Distribution Centre,
Colchester Road, Frating Green, Colchester, Essex, CO7 7DW
E-mail: customerservice@ospreypublishing.com

www.ospreypublishing.com

CONTENTS

UNION INFANTRYMAN
1861–65

HISTORICAL BACKGROUND

The United States census for 1860 reported that 31,443,321 people called the vast young nation home, a substantial increase from the previous decade when the count was 23,191,876. Some four million of these people were foreign-born, arriving from Great Britain, Europe, or far away China to seek opportunities in a new land. A very similar number of the country's inhabitants, or more usually their ancestors, had been forced to the United States from Africa, unfortunate souls who were enslaved in the supposed land of the free. Most of them labored long and hard in the South.

A Union field grade officer (majors, lieutenant-colonels, and colonels) in the double-breasted dark blue frock coat with seven buttons in each row to indicate his status. The forage cap with sloping visor on the table sometimes is referred to as the "McDowell" pattern. (USAMHI)

2nd Lt. John K. Clary of the 14th U.S. Infantry poses in the uniform typical of a company grade (second lieutenants, first lieutenants, and captains) infantry officer's uniform consisting of a dark blue nine-button frock coat with shoulder straps, sky-blue trousers with dark blue ⅛ in. welt, and forage cap bearing a hunting horn insignia. (USAMHI)

In the North, fully 58 percent of the population still lived and worked on farms, many of which were small family-owned affairs. The remainder of Northern residents flocked to cities, which began to mushroom across the countryside as urbanization and industrialization increasingly spread from New York to Chicago and beyond. More and more, the Southerners with their rural "slaveocracy" grew apart from their urban Yankee factory-working brethren. The gulf steadily widened between the two regions, so much so that it seemed the nation could not exist "half slave and half free."

The long simmering discord between those who lived in the North and the South had occasionally approached boiling point. But with the election of Abraham Lincoln as 16th president of the United States, the lid finally blew off the kettle. Several Southern states seceded to form the Confederacy. Northern states united under the Stars and Stripes. On April 12 1861, Southern artillerymen defiantly fired on Fort Sumter, an island-based brick bastion in Charleston harbor, South Carolina. For the next 30 hours gunners mercilessly pounded this target, intent on bringing about the surrender of the federal fortress. The American Civil War had begun.

Both sides thought the conflict would be short-lived; both believed they were in the right and would soon prevail. Convictions ran high, turning friend against friend, brother against brother, son against father.

CHRONOLOGY

1860
6 November Abraham Lincoln elected president of the United States.
20 December South Carolina secedes from the Union.

1861
18 February Jefferson Davis inaugurated as president of the Confederate States of America.
12 April Gen. P. G. T. Beauregard orders the attack on Fort Sumter.
15 April Lincoln calls upon the loyal states to furnish 75,000 volunteers.
21 July first battle of Bull Run (Manassas).
10 August battle of Wilson's Creek. Union retains control of Missouri.

1862
23 March battle of Kernstown.
6–7 April battle of Shiloh.
25 May 3,000 Union men lost at the first battle of Winchester.
25 June–1 July The "Seven Days" is waged with Robert E. Lee in retreat, but Richmond is saved from attack.
29–30 August second battle of Bull Run.
17 September battle of Antietam (Sharpsburg) temporarily shifts the war to the north.
22 September Lincoln issues the Emancipation Proclamation to free the enslaved blacks held in those states engaged in the rebellion.
13 December battle of Fredericksburg.

1863
1–4 May battle of Chancellorsville.
13–15 June Confederates route Union forces at second battle of Winchester.
1–3 July battle of Gettysburg, considered by many the "high water mark of the Confederacy".
19 November Lincoln delivers the Gettysburg Address.
24 November battle of Lookout Mountain.

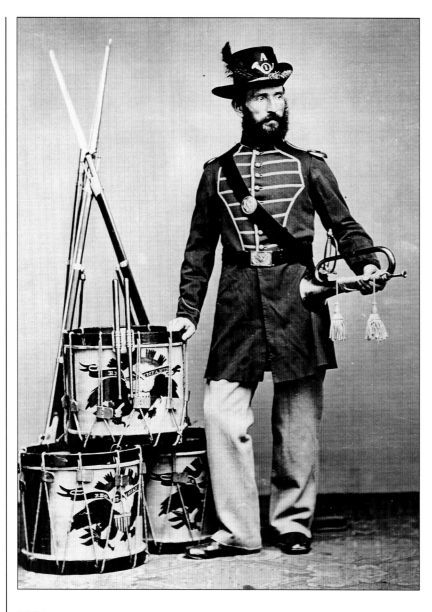

LEFT **The regulation U.S. Army infantry musician's uniform as prescribed in 1861 with sky-blue trousers. The lace on the frock coat was sky blue, the color prescribed for infantry trim. (SI)**

A proud private of Company C, 17th U.S. Infantry, one of the new Regular Army regiments formed soon after the Civil War began, appears in the regulation dress uniform of enlisted men, although he has creased his headgear in a non-regulation manner to give it the appearance of a so-called "Burnside" hat. (MM)

1864

9 March Ulysses S. Grant appointed general–in-chief to command in the field.

5–6 May battle of Wilderness.

8–12 May battle of Spotsylvania.

15 June–2 April 1865 siege of Petersburg and Richmond.

27 June battle of Kenesaw Mountain.

2 September William T. Sherman captures Atlanta.

19 September–9 October third battle of Winchester.

15 November Sherman begins his march to the sea.

15–16 December battle of Nashville.

1865

17 February Sherman's men occupy Columbia, SC.

3 April Richmond surrenders.

9 April Lee surrenders to Grant at Appomattox Courthouse.

14 April Lincoln assassinated.

26 April Joseph Johnston surrenders to William Sherman at Greensboro, NC, bringing the war to an end.

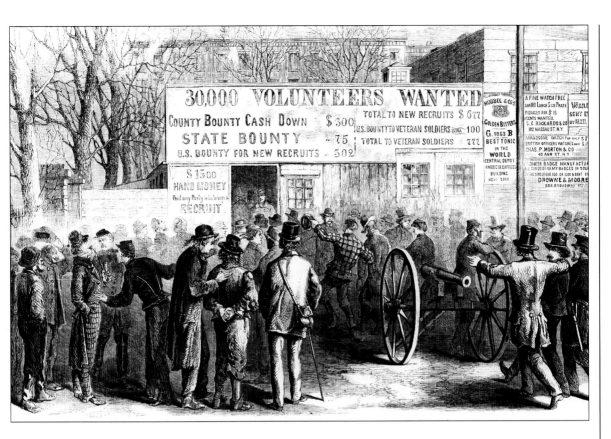

Will you join the ranks to save the Union? Abraham Lincoln required a military organization much larger than the tiny Regular Army to put down the rebellion. (LC USZ62-93555)

RECRUITMENT

After the opening salvos at Fort Sumter support for the war ran wild. At first recruiting proved easy. One enthusiastic disciple of retaliation spoke for many when he asked: "What is a man's life worth if our glorious union is to be shattered by traitors?"

In the beginning, tens of thousands of Northerners enthusiastically rallied to Lincoln's call on April 15 (under the Militia Act of 1792) for 75,000 volunteers to sign on for three months service. Each state received a quota based on its population, and there was little difficulty in supplying the numbers required. Many flocked to the colors: some were born in the United States; others came from abroad, and units made up of Italians, sons of Eire, those of Germanic or Norwegian stock and others vied to display loyalty to their new country. No matter what their origins, patriotic fervor, a chance for adventure, financial benefits, and other motives made it appear that the tiny U.S. Army of some 16,000 men would be swamped by floods of reinforcements from the zealous citizenry.

Ohioan Sheldon Colton was one of those who answered the president's call. Before the war erupted he had been working for an insurance company. When word came that the Regular Army was to be expanded by 22,714 officers and men, which ultimately included the addition of nine new infantry regiments to bolster the existing ten, Colton considered throwing in his lot with one of the new units. There was one proviso: he only would do so if he could receive a commission.

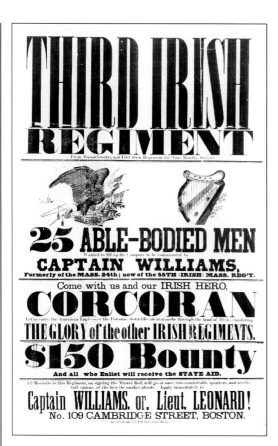

THIRD IRISH REGIMENT

From Massachusetts, and First Irish Regiment for Nine Months Service.

25 ABLE-BODIED MEN

Wanted to fill up the Company to be commanded by

CAPTAIN WILLIAMS,

Formerly of the MASS. 24th; now of the 55TH (IRISH) MASS. REG'T.

Come with us and our IRISH HERO,

CORCORAN

Let us carry the American Eagle over the Potomac, down like an avalanche through the land of Dixie, emulating

THE GLORY of the other IRISH REGIMENTS.

$150 Bounty

And all who Enlist will receive the STATE AID.

All Recruits to this Regiment, on signing the Muster Roll, will go at once into comfortable quarters, and receive full rations of the best the market affords. Apply immediately to

Captain WILLIAMS, or. Lieut. LEONARD!

No. 109 CAMBRIDGE STREET, BOSTON.

Although recruiting proved easy at the beginning of the war, as the conflict continued a number of inducements had to be found to entice recruits for the Union, including the offering of cash bounties, as in this poster for the 3rd Irish Regiment. (LC USZ62-40807)

He told his parents that a company of the 14th U.S. Infantry was forming in the vicinity with several "able men – some of them old military men", and he wanted to be among their number. It seemed that health problems might render him unfit as a common soldier, but he believed he could serve as an officer and that the outdoor life of a military man even would afford him "an increase of strength."

He saw other advantages to a commission. For one thing, unlike the common soldier who would enlist for a specified period of time, an officer could resign and return home if he desired, or so Colton thought. Although the role might be "a little more dangerous on the field, but not much," chances were he might not even see combat, but instead be stationed "at some fort during the entire campaign." Moreover, when not on duty "he would have plenty of time to read and study."

He further speculated he could earn from $50 to $75 per month, which was far more than a private's pay of $13 a month (raised to $16 a month in May 1864). As such, he could send money home to help his parents and sisters who remained behind. Another economic motive stemmed from Colton's concern for the consequences if the war proved a prolonged one. He envisioned that this would prostrate the country and have dire economic consequences that would adversely impact his family's financial situation. But not all his motives were tied to fiscal matters. His letter related: "I would like to do what I can for my country in the present crisis, and have but little of the 'sinews of war' at my command. I have an ordinary amount of sinews of body, however, a cool head, and plenty of warm blood to spare if necessary. I hope I have enough courage to stand fire, but cannot till I am tried, as I have never been in any very dangerous positions."

Colton added he was not afraid to die, did not worry greatly about pain, nor seek glory because he did not think "there would be much, and I am not particularly anxious for Military fame." In this telling piece of correspondence the prospective soldier revealed the extent of sentiments that were shared in varying degrees by many of those who responded to the call to arms.

In the end, though, he did not carry out his first course of action to become a Regular. He was not alone: by December 1861 just 20,334 individuals made up the permanent part of Lincoln's army, representing only a small increase over the antebellum numbers. The fact that enlistment in this force was for three years did much to keep the numbers small, as did certain prejudices in Congress and elsewhere against a large standing army. By that same time, in contrast 640,000 volunteers had entered the Northern war machine. The state troops and volunteers would continue to dominate; by March 31 1862 the Regulars totaled only 23,308 artillery, cavalry, infantry, and support troops, as opposed to 613,818 volunteers and a substantial number of militiamen. It was not surprising then that Colton followed the norm when he decided to join the 67th Ohio Volunteer Infantry.

Here again he took a path that was not dissimilar to many hundreds or thousands of others. As the new unit formed, Colton opined that the regiment would be filled with good men and recruiting would be easy as "war fever" was "pretty strong" in the area. With that analysis he decided he would "have a pretty fair chance of raising a company" of foot soldiers and even could be the captain if he wished, but did "not exactly like to take the responsibility of doing so, until I am better acquainted with the duties of the place."

While uncertain of his quest for a captaincy, Colton had no doubts about becoming an officer. With this goal in mind he ordered a uniform blouse in preparation for his appointment. By November his supposition proved correct when he was commissioned a second lieutenant. At this point he had enticed 13 men to enlist in his company, although slightly later he found that enthusiasm waned and his prospects of gathering 30 souls seemed unlikely. He confessed, "One needs all the patience of which a man was ever possessed to keep his temper and listen to excuses of able bodied young men who are asked to enlist."

Among those he hoped to add was a youth who had gone off to obtain his mother's written consent. In this case, despite a desire to round up more men, Colton demonstrated a commitment to observe the age restriction unlike some other recruiters. Apparently some anxious boys placed pieces of paper in their shoes with the number "18" scribbled on the scraps or wrote the figure on the soles of their footwear so that they could swear that they were "over eighteen" when asked if they met the minimum age requirement. In more than one case this statement went unchallenged. Some sources estimate 200,000 recruits did not give their correct age, but inflated it by a year or so, while a few even claimed they were younger so that they would not be rejected for being too old. Such was the case of Curtis King, a hardy octogenarian who was on the rolls of the 37th Iowa Infantry for a few months. Peer-pressure accounted for much of this behavior, or so Samuel Merrill of the 70th Indiana assumed: "Nine-tenths of them enlisted just because somebody else was going, and the other tenth was ashamed to stay at home."

This meant that there were many 16 or 17 year olds in the ranks who had circumvented the age requirement. Excited by the stories of the valor of the 1st Iowa Volunteer Infantry at the battle of Wilson Creek, Missouri, the average age of some 97 youths who signed up for the new 11th Iowa was under 20.

Even younger lads managed to enroll, typically as musicians. One of these was John Clem, a native of Newark, Ohio. In May 1861, before his 10th birthday, Clem supposedly tried to become a drummer with the 3rd Ohio Volunteers, but was rejected. Undaunted, he quickly tried again, this time tagging along with the 22nd Michigan Volunteer Infantry. Almost a year later he was with the regiment in Tennessee where his proven coolness under fire at the battle of Shiloh earned him the nickname of "Johnny Shiloh". By September 1863, at Chickamauga, the plucky Clem was said to have wounded a Confederate colonel, then took the man prisoner. Although Clem was but 12 at the time, he received a promotion to sergeant. Ultimately Clem would be wounded twice, taken as a prisoner of war, and released by the rebels in 1864, all by the time he was 14. With that, the seasoned veteran went back to Ohio to attend high school!

Alson Ostrander was another adolescent who wanted to be admitted into the ranks. When he was three the impressionable boy had been placed on the knee of his venerable great-grand-father, a Revolutionary War veteran who still had his flintlock musket propped next to him as he rocked on the porch of the family home. Ostrander's father further fueled the flames by telling him stories of the Revolution, while a neighbor who had served in the Mexican War took him to West Point on several occasions. These influences and the writings of James Fenimore Cooper led Alson to reveal in his later autobiography: "Is there any wonder why that I was eager for a chance to be a soldier?"

At first his father insisted that Alson was too young to consider leaving school for the military. He bowed to his father's wishes for a time, and even took advantage of an offer to study at Eastman's Commercial College in New York (a vocational institution where clerks learnt practical skills). After six months he secured a clerkship in the local provost marshal's office. In due course the officer in charge asked if Ostrander wanted "to go into the army". Receiving an enthusiastic affirmative, Alson was told to bring his father around the next day.

After he went home he recounted the events of this interview with his father. Finally he heard the words he longed for. If he were determined to enlist his father would give his blessing so long as Alson would go into the Regulars; the necessary papers were signed the next day. Soon the anxious stripling was off to the barracks at Governor's Island in New York City. There he was marched down to the part of the garrison where the "music boys were quartered" and asked whether he preferred to "learn to be a drummer or a fifer". He elected for the latter, and so began his military career at barely 15 years of age.

As part of the process Ostrander had undergone a complete medical examination. This was not necessarily common during the early phases of the war. In fact, the medical inspection often was so lax that no fewer than 400 women were known to have enlisted without their gender being discovered. These were departures from the norm, however. The typical Union foot soldier was a white male between the ages of 18 and 29. He was Protestant and single for the most part, although he came from at least one of 300 different occupations. Furthermore, the majority were native born. Of the two million or so Union troops, perhaps 75 percent listed their birthplace in the United States. The rest came from various parts of Germany (175,000), Ireland (150,000), Britain (45,000), and Canada (15,000), while another 75,000 had arrived from other places, including a few of Chinese descent.

Besides diversity in places of origin, there was an assortment of sizes as well. Despite a minimum height requirement of 5 ft 3 in. one enlisted

Nine-year-old John Clem was one of many boys who joined the Northern infantry. By war's end he had become a sergeant. (LC B8184-10345)

man of the 192nd Ohio stood only 3 ft 4 in. – tiny compared to Captain David Van Buskirk of the 27th Indiana Volunteer Infantry, a giant for the time of 6 ft 11 in. and 380 pounds as opposed to most Union soldiers who were in the 110 to 220 pound range.

Renewing the ranks

Not only were individuals of varying heights and weights accepted, but men were also admitted with diverse physical abilities. Aged, deformed, deaf, and diseased inductees were passed into the ranks by uncaring or unknowing physicians. Such slipshod practices had repercussions that could sometimes be disastrous. At best, the arduous life in field and campaign made these unhealthy specimens candidates for discharge or doctor's treatment. At worst, death took them from the ranks without them ever hearing an enemy musket fired.

Writing from Camp Lincoln in Keokuck, Iowa, Private Newton Scott of Company A, the 36th Iowa Volunteer Infantry, summed up this predicament in a scribbled note to a loved one at home: "there are thousands of Poor Soldiers that will see Home & Friends no more in this World. If you was in Keokuck & see the numbers of Sick & Disabled Soldiers it would make your Heart Ache."

This was not an unusual state of affairs and by late 1862 some 200,000 recruits had been released after proving physically unfit for service. Reforms followed requiring stiffer guidelines for admission, and more thorough examinations.

When insufficient volunteers rallied to the call for additional troops, the federal government instituted a draft. Names were picked randomly and the men selected were summoned to duty. (LC USZ62-46372)

The draft outraged some Northerners and even led to riots in a few instances, such as in New York City where colored people particularly became scapegoats of outrage. (LC USZ62-41234)

The loss of manpower did not end there. For one thing, a number of the original volunteers had agreed to 90 days in uniform, and afterwards were free to leave. Even those who had been taken in for longer terms of six months, a year, two years or three (the length varied with time and circumstances, a consistent period never being adopted during the war) left when their stint was over. This fluctuation constantly challenged Yankee leaders to replenish the force. Indeed, the Union never developed an adequate replacement system, but attempted several measures to supply personnel as the war raged on.

As early as July 1861 Lincoln realized his initial requirement for troops would not be sufficient, so he requested another half-million volunteers to join for from six months to three years as the president saw fit to define the obligation. In his recollections about service with the 14th New Hampshire Volunteer Infantry, one of the three-year units, F. H. Buffum summed up the type of individuals who continued to rally to the Union cause after the period of initial enthusiasm waned. He wrote: "The men who responded were not Bohemians, nor mere seekers for a better fortune. They were mostly fixtures in society ... They were men who could not have been bought from wife, children, and the family home of generations for one hundred or one thousand dollars. And such men were the overwhelming majority of the three-years' volunteers of 1862."

While these stout fellows proved the backbone of the Federal force, finding willing individuals to respond to this and subsequent recruiting efforts presented more and more problems as the war dragged on. By March 1863 the United States Congress passed the Enrollment Act, which introduced the first nationwide conscription, a practice that the South already had resorted to. All white males between the ages of 20 and 45 were eligible for the draft. If called, a conscript would be committed to three years in uniform.

There were several ways to avoid induction. A man could pay a $300 commutation compensation when his name was drawn to gain exemption. Another way to keep from being called up was to hire a substitute. In both cases, those with the economic wherewithal could evade the draft; poorer men could not. This caused discontent and accusations that the Enrollment Act was a "rich man's bill," but a poor man's fight. In 1864 further legislation withdrew the commutation option, but kept substitution in place. Exemption was also possible for men who were in poor health, whose family would experience hardship, or who could demonstrate religious grounds for remaining out of the service.

In addition, if a draftee resided in a county that had filled its quota, regardless of his financial standing, he was also safe. This was simply because the draft did not apply to such areas. Sometimes local governments would try to reach the required quota of volunteers by offering bounties, cash bonuses or promises of a lump sum in addition to regular pay at the end of service. These inducements, along with

Some men avoided service by paying a substitute to go in their place, a practice that artist Adalbert Volck ridiculed for a Southern audience in his *Confederate War Etchings*. Many Northerners likewise looked askance at this option to avoid entering the military. (LC USZ62-31202)

shorter periods of enlistment for volunteers, lured many prospective soldiers into the ranks. Some communities were so intent on providing the necessary manpower that they competed with one another, and with the federal government in some instances to attract recruits. The incentives ran as high as $1,000 in a few cases, a sum that was many times the annual wage of the average unskilled worker or farmer.

Despite loopholes, not everyone could find a means to escape conscription. The very idea rankled some, and generally the practice tended to be disdained. Even a number of military leaders balked because they thought anyone who had been forced into the army would make an inadequate combatant. There even were demonstrations against conscription and the *Washington Times* reported, "The nation is at this time in a state of Revolution, North, South, East, and West." While this report was overstated, people in some places, especially New York City, did react adversely. After the names of the city's first draftees appeared in newspapers on July 11 1863 this information and the recent losses at Gettysburg combined as a violent catalyst. A riot broke out that lasted for three days. Looting, destruction of property, beatings, and even lynching occurred as a mob of some 50,000 took to the streets.

Many of the perpetrators were Irish, while several of the victims were colored. This situation went beyond the powerful racism of the period, which was summed up to a certain degree by the saying: "We ain't for the Nigger, but we are for the war." The situation was worsened by the fact that the Irish, who were on the lowest rungs of the economic ladder, vied with African Americans for jobs albeit menial and low paying ones. A number of immigrants from Ireland now thought they were being unfairly singled out for military service, while blacks would remain behind in safety to gain employment, a path that was open to them because African Americans had been barred from enlisting soon after the war began.

After the riots were quelled by militiamen and troops rushed from the Army of the Potomac to New York, disdain for the draft prevailed. Little wonder, then, that draftees made up only about two percent of the entire Union army, and substitutes (an estimated 118,000 men) accounted for approximately 18 percent of Yankee soldiery.

Ironically, blacks comprised one of the groups exempted from the draft. During the early years of the war Lincoln resisted pressure from a number of sectors advocating the enlistment of African Americans. Runaway slaves, frequently known as "contrabands", were sometimes hired as laborers to free fighting forces from non-combatant roles. All this ended when the Emancipation Proclamation went into effect on January 1 1863. Previously those blacks who had sought service did so without the sanction of Washington. Nonetheless, by the conclusion of the war approximately 180,000 black soldiers, mostly members of the U.S. Colored Troops (U.S.C.T.), had fought for their freedom, a prize earned by blood rather than given as a gift. Of these, nearly 40,000 died. The majority had cast off the bonds of slavery, but several units were made up largely of free blacks, one of the most famous of these outfits being the 54th Massachusetts Volunteer Infantry. By war's end, nearly 10 percent of the total Union Army's strength were African Americans.

"NO PLASTER SAINTS": SOLDIER LIFE

Regardless of background or how they came to find themselves in the army, few new recruits had any idea of what they were about to face. The majority had never served in the military, or had been more than a few miles away from their homes, at least in the cases of thousands of native-born lads. More often than not, they at least had their neighbors and friends with them, some even showing up with family members.

Conversely, some units had been formed from as many as 15 nationalities. In such cases it was not unusual to have men who spoke or understood little or no English. At times there were drawbacks to such diversity. Lt. Colton complained: "I have more trouble than the law will allow with the Germans connected with the band."

This was not the only example of discordance that was so characteristic in the early days of the war. As another illustration of the disarray uniforms seem to have come in all the colors of the rainbow. Typically, the new recruits started in civilian attire, sometimes shoeless. After that the volunteers might be given complete outfits or pieces of their uniform, thereby mixing civilian and martial clothing. Styles varied from unit to unit, and inconsistencies from one company to another in the same regiment were not uncommon.

Headgear types varied widely for Union infantrymen. While the forage cap was worn extensively, the fez-like stocking caps donned by three members of the 23rd New York Volunteer Infantry represent just one variation on the theme. Note the soldier seated on the left cleans his mess plate, while his comrade in the center writes in a journal. (NA)

These three members of 23rd New York Volunteer Infantry Regiment are armed with Enfield muskets to which they have affixed the distinctive sword or saber bayonet. At the outset of the war the unit was issued gray trousers, frock coats, and forage caps, but changed over to a dark blue jacket piped in light blue later in the conflict, as did many other units. (NA)

Educational levels tended to be low, with a portion of the recruits not even knowing their left foot from their right. This was not always the case, however: the 33rd Illinois Volunteer Infantry, for example, had an officer corps that was filled with professors and teachers.

Whatever the individual background and reasons for joining, once an individual reported for duty as a soldier, a chain of events was set into motion that was supposed to transform him and his comrades into a fighting force. For one thing the men had to be assembled, then usually they were moved to another location. This might be accomplished on foot or via railroads, a network of which existed throughout much of the North. Some were fortunate enough to be transported in passenger cars; others rode freight cars. On occasion ships were used to move the units down the coast to Washington, DC, and beyond.

Another basic requirement was to see to the necessities of sustaining the troops, feeding, clothing and sheltering them. Quartermaster and commissary personnel dealt rather hastily and inadequately with rations, and in the early days components of civilian garb and military items were often mixed together. Even later, there was no consistency in uniforms, but by the middle of the war certain items such as the plain four-button dark blue flannel sack coat and sky-blue kersey trousers dominated. Furthermore, headgear ranged from the old 1858-pattern

15

The 2nd Rhode Island Volunteer Infantry wore a distinct blouse that resembled a blue smock, as Capt. Cyrus Dyer of the regiment illustrates. Uniform variations were common during the early years of the war. (MM)

black issue hat, to forage caps of differing styles, to a conglomeration of civilian slouch hats and straw hats depending on climate and availability.

As far as shelter was concerned, men might bed down in the open atop a blanket or some sort of ground cloth. Sheldon Colton noted that he had carried an enameled blanket for this purpose, but soon exchanged it for a rubber one, which was "in reality a piano cover". The men also could pair up with a comrade and pitch a *Tente d'Abri* that also was styled a shelter tent or "dog" tent. This was a piece of waterproofed cotton drilling or other heavy material, available in two pieces. Each man might carry half a tent section measuring roughly 5 ft 2 in. by 4 ft 8 in. Two sections were buttoned together and suspended from a guy line stretched between trees, or even a pair of muskets thrust into the ground with their bayonets affixed.

A wedge or "A" tent could also be erected, with a capacity from four to six men. Supplied with upright poles, they were carried by baggage wagons and tended to form part of permanent camps, rather than be set up for armies on the move. The Sibley tent was an even larger circular 12-man shelter that resembled a Native American teepee. A cone-shaped stove could be placed in the middle of this lodging for heating.

None of these options offered adequate protection from inclement weather. Winter specifically dictated other arrangements. Sometimes local civilian structures might be found to protect the men from the elements. More usually, the men turned to their own resources and constructed winter quarters from logs, stone, branches, and whatever else they might be able to press into service to help relieve their lot.

Organization

The main tactical element of the Union infantry was the regiment. In volunteer units there were ten companies lettered from A to K, excluding the letter J. While this was the typical arrangement, early in the war some of the new Regular Army infantry regiments were to be composed of from two to three battalions, each with ten companies. In April 1861 the strength for all companies in volunteer regiments was set at between 64 and 82 privates, with one wagoner, two musicians, eight corporals, four sergeants, a first sergeant, a second lieutenant, a first lieutenant, and a captain making up the remainder of the contingent.

At the start of the war the rank and file volunteers often elected the junior officers, a custom that had both strengths and weaknesses, but was not uncommon. Later, a system of examinations was introduced in an effort to determine potential leaders with ability. This concept did not gain total acceptance, however.

Another convention inaugurated early in the war, but which remained unchanged despite the fact that it had less than satisfactory results, was the replacement system for losses. Rather than send recruits into old units to restore depleted strengths as the Confederates did, the Union created new regiments. This meant that veteran organizations often dwindled far below the minimum of 845 prescribed by regulations. In his *Numbers and Losses in the Civil War in America*, Thomas Livermore concluded federal regiments averaged 560 effectives at Shiloh; 650 at Fair Oaks; 530 at Chancellorsville; and only 375 at Gettysburg. Another study stated that at Gettysburg company strength averaged only 32 officers and enlisted personnel. Some regiments

literally fought themselves out of existence, a situation which devastated morale and adversely impacted on combat readiness.

These reduced strengths meant that in several cases federal brigades, which were supposed to consist of four or five regiments, actually had little more than that total required to fill a regiment. In turn, two or more brigades were combined into divisions, with an average of approximately 6,200 infantrymen. At the next echelon two or more divisions regularly made up a corps commanded by a major-general. In the Army of the Potomac there were around 16,000 troops in a corps of men from the assorted arms and support services. Finally, the largest Union operational unit was the army (each was named after a river) of

The single line formation of a regiment early in the war was more compact than the later extended order arrangement, that employed skirmishers in front and successive companies behind. Improved weapons, munition and entrenched positions dictated such a change in tactics.

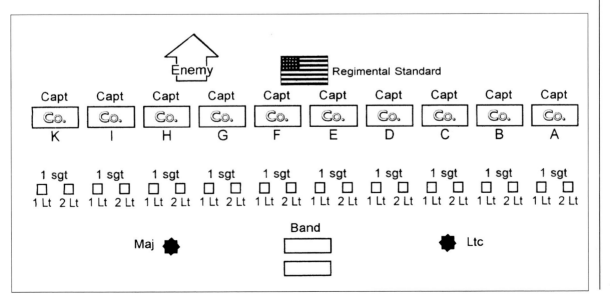

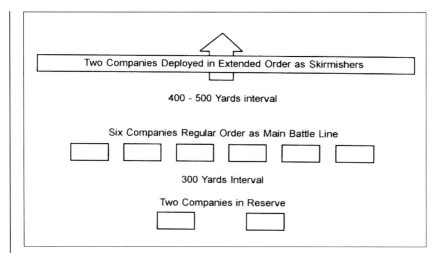

Two Companies Deployed in Extended Order as Skirmishers

400 - 500 Yards interval

Six Companies Regular Order as Main Battle Line

300 Yards Interval

Two Companies in Reserve

The typical tactical deployment of an infantry regiment arrayed for combat. This grew from the realization that rifled muskets were devastating to the close order formations employed at the beginning of the war.

which there were 16 in existence at various times during the war. They were usually formed from various combinations of corps and divisions.

Tactics

Tactics that had changed little from the American Revolution and the Napoleonic era originally dictated how these forces would be deployed. During the first engagements of the war, Federal commanders still used a close order linear formation advancing behind a line of skirmishers, delivering massed volley fire, then driving home the assault with bayonets. This formula worked reasonably well in the age of short-range smoothbores, but was disastrous by the time of the Civil War because of the combination of rifling and improved ammunition. At battles such as Fredericksburg this cruel lesson was learned through body counts. Union attackers at Marye's Heights piled up over 100 yards from the Confederate lines, with few of their number reaching closer than 50 to 100 yards of the rebels.

Observant Union officers, including Brig. Gen. Emory Upton, concluded that they would have to open the lines of infantry to achieve success. Large numbers of skirmishers were to take the advance and do so rapidly in order to cut the time of exposure to enemy fire. The trick was not to disperse too much, so that sufficient strength was available to overrun the foe once the objective had been reached. Upton's answer to this balancing act was to send in four waves, the first to lead the way; the second to occupy the former enemy positions; the third to lie down behind the second line as a ready reserve, while the fourth waited at the start point to react to the situation. While all this made sense, most officers clung to the tactics developed before the war.

Another alteration in thinking that began to achieve slow acceptance was the use of entrenchments. Defense, including elaborate fortifications at times, gained importance even as direct advancing formations from the age of Napoleon diminished and all but disappeared. Digging in was not only important in infantry-against-infantry clashes, but also when artillery was involved. By 1864 this procedure had become standard.

Tactics for repelling cavalry attacks also harkened back to early times. Once again, the range and reliability of firearms in the hands of foot soldiers made specialized drill formations such as the square unnecessary.

The shirt-blouse of this private of the 2nd Rhode Island Volunteer Infantry is less tailored than that worn by Capt. Dyer. Typically, enlisted uniforms were not of as high quality as those worn by officers.

Training

In order to implement tactics the soldiery had to become adept at drill. Training fell to the officers and NCOs, who possessed varied backgrounds and capabilities.

To aid these leaders General Orders No. 13, War Department, February 11 1862 called for each infantry regiment to be provided with 35 volumes of *Army Regulations* (the "blue book"), 35 of tactics, 30 covering bayonet exercises, and a like number relative to outpost duties. On the surface, issue of these tomes seemed to be a good idea, but because there were several versions of the manuals the outcome was not always as desired. Gen. Winfield Scott's three-volume manual dating from the mid-1830s might be applied in some units, while the two-volume *Rifle and Infantry Tactics* of the 1850s by the former commandant of the U.S. Military Academy turned Confederate general William J. Hardee might be utilized in another outfit. (It was revised early in the war and taken up by Southerners.) Other publications existed, too, which some officers obtained in an effort to master the military profession. Ultimately Brig. Gen. Silas Casey's three-volume compilation attempted to make sense out of all this, and Lincoln approved this publication on August 11 1862 for all infantry "whether Regular, Volunteer, or Militia". As an illustration of the state of affairs even West Pointer William T. Sherman, who had left the army not long after the Mexican–American War, had to go back to the basics after he reentered the service in 1861.

If former military men were befuddled, the incoming legions of one-time clerks, politicians, bankers, and lawyers, who had received commissions as company- and field-grade officers, must have been daunted by the prospects of learning their new trade and passing it on to their men. To varying degrees, some of the more energetic mastered all or part of what they had to in order to prepare their men, who typically started their military education by learning facings. From there

This young infantryman sports the single breasted sky-blue kersey overcoat with short attached cape commonly issued to foot soldiers in the Union Army. The pattern dated back to the previous decade. (MM)

Union infantrymen had to be resourceful. A man in the ubiquitous sky-blue kersey foot soldier's overcoat has converted a cigar box into a fiddle, while the canvas field tent is reinforced by logs plastered with clay and heated with a makeshift fireplace and chimney topped with a plowshare. This was added to keep the smoke from blowing back into the shelter. (LC USZ62-14188)

In the vicinity of Fallmouth, Virginia Union soldiers build a chimney as part of their winter quarters. (LC USZ62-9271)

they might progress to more intricate formation changes that could be continued for six to eight hours daily.

One less than zealous recruit found this routine boring. He decided to express his dissatisfaction to the instructor, and walked over to state: "Let's stop this fooling around and go over to the grocery." The sergeant turned to the complaining man's corporal and after some choice

A group of infantry NCOs and officers relax in a winter camp, complete with wooden boardwalks to keep them from walking in the mud. Soldiers did what they could to create rudimentary creature comforts. (NA)

expletives the unenthusiastic soldier was treated to a prolonged individual session to help him understand the importance of drill.

The protesting pupil was just one of hundreds of thousands who marched and wheeled repeatedly at squad level at first; if there was time, company and even regimental instruction ensued. The results differed from unit to unit, depending on the competence of leadership at various levels and the aptitude of their subordinates. One new infantryman was not impressed with his outfit and observed that he had "not joined an army, but an unprepared mob". Such rudimentary training was better than none at all, yet some units went directly into combat without receiving even basic instructions as soldiers.

Even if a company mastered the complexities, its men still had to learn how to operate at the regimental, brigade, and corps level. Each echelon required more knowledge than might be able to be absorbed prior to going into combat.

Marksmanship

Unfamiliarity with firearms as a military weapon was another challenge to those who attempted to transform civilians into fighting men. Col. Oliver Spaulding made an observation of the 23rd Michigan that probably applied to the majority of Union infantry regiments: "Quite a number of men had never fired a gun in their lives, and several of them, when commanded to fire, would shut their eyes, turn their heads in the opposite direction, and blaze away." One solution was for the War Department to reprint Willard's *System of Target Practice* during 1862. This set of instructions set up a course that began with practice in loading, sighting, and aiming with blank cartridges. Next, the men were to shoot live ammunition beginning with individual firing, then moving on to platoon and company levels.

When it came time to rouse the camp, drummers or other bandsmen awakened their fellow infantrymen. Are the troops about to start another day of routine drill, or are they to march against the enemy? (LC USZ62-33832)

Napoleonic-era tactics were still in use when the Civil War erupted, including the formation of a square to repel cavalry, being demonstrated here by the 139th Pennsylvania Volunteer Infantry Regiment. (LC B8164-B-306)

BELOW Several versions of manuals existed during the war, making it difficult for officers and their subordinates to settle on a consistent form of drill. Most of the publications shared at least one thing in common – line drawings depicting many of the basics for foot soldiers. (USAMHI)

Marksmanship often seemed less important than speed. Some statistics reveal the fallacy of that approach. During July 1862, at Murfreesboro, Tennessee, the Yankees unleashed 145 rounds for every Rebel they hit, while the next month at Gainesville, Virginia, 100 bullets were expended for every wounded or killed member of the opposition. Almost two years later Capt. Samuel Fiske of the 14th Connecticut Volunteer Infantry added another comment condemning the federal practice of teaching recruits "to load and fire as rapidly as possible, three or four times a minute; they go about their business with all fury, every man vying with his neighbor as to the number of cartridges he can ram into his piece." Then the air became so filled with smoke that nothing could be seen as a target, and "by and by the guns get heated, and won't go off, and the cartridges begin to give out." The idea at this point was not for precision firing, but instead to throw as much lead at the enemy as possible.

But Fiske disdained this approach. "Practice? If I had charge of a regiment or brigade," he wrote, "I'd put every man in the guard-house who could be proved to have fired more than twenty rounds in one battle."

Ammunition and weapons

While the Connecticut infantry officer decried practices or random, rapid fire, the fact is that this method had considerable effect. One Confederate fighting at the Hornet's Nest (so-called because of the near constant buzzing of bullets fired by both sides) during the battle of Shiloh likened his experience to the enemy feeding "us Minié balls for breakfast". In this instance the Rebel soldier was referring to a type of bullet perfected in 1848 by the French army officer Capt. Claude Etienne Minié. The Minié ball had a hollowed-out base that expanded when the gunpowder behind it ignited, forcing the conical lead shell to fit more tightly into the rifling of the barrel for greater accuracy and distance. Named after its inventor, the device gave infantrymen more accurate killing power at longer ranges than ever before, and became a fearful presence on the battlefield. The devastating effects of lead on flesh could be illustrated by the example of the first sergeant of Company A of the 2nd New Hampshire Volunteer Infantry, who at the battle of Cold Harbor, Virginia (May 31–June 12 1864) was struck by one of these bullets in the right arm, which splintered the bone into 23 pieces.

Some explosive bullets were also available during the war, although they were issued only on a very limited basis. For instance, during the summer of 1863 the 2nd New Hampshire Volunteer Infantry received "forty cartridges per man" of what were "called musket-shells—an explosive bullet", of which the regimental history later warned "woe to the Johnny that stops one!"

Indeed, if hit by one of these rounds the results could be ghastly, but the enemy was not the only one who might be in danger from this volatile ammunition. When the 2nd New Hampshire went into action at Gettysburg, enemy artillery fire ripped into a cartridge box of a corporal in Company C. For 30 seconds the eruptive contents went off directly into the unfortunate man's quaking body. Death was almost instantaneous. When a sergeant in the unit was struck in a similar manner, he managed to extract himself from his bursting pouch in time to sustain an intense wound, but at least he survived.

It was not only the ammunition that could turn combat into a feast of death. Rifled weapons, which eventually became the mainstay of the Federal foot soldier, although not completely replacing smoothbores, increased the precision and reach of the common foot soldier. Individual sharpshooters or special units made up of skilled marksmen, such as the 1st Regiment U.S. Sharpshooters (Berdan's) armed with breechloading .52 caliber Sharps rifles, could wreak even greater havoc among enemy troop formations.

The Union foot soldier was beset with a bewildering inventory of weapons. In all, some four million small arms were issued to Union troops during the war. They included everything from outdated converted flintlock muzzle-loading, single-shoot .69 caliber muskets, to metallic cartridge magazine arms such as the .44 caliber Henry

A

SYSTEM

OF

TARGET PRACTICE.

FOR THE USE OF TROOPS

WHEN ARMED WITH THE MUSKET, RIFLE-MUSKET, RIFLE, OR CARBINE.

PREPARED PRINCIPALLY FROM THE FRENCH.

PUBLISHED BY ORDER OF THE WAR DEPARTMENT.

WASHINGTON:
GOVERNMENT PRINTING OFFICE.
1862.

The average Union infantryman had limited experience with firearms and had to be taught to shoot, sometimes following Willard's *System of Target Practice*. (USAMHI)

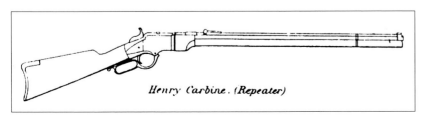

Henry Carbine. (Repeater)

The Henry was among the weapons that fired metallic cartridges. This lever action repeater had a 16-round capacity. (USAMHI)

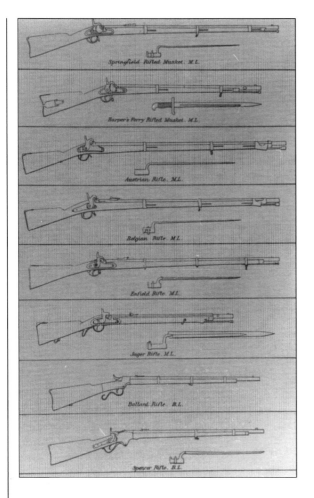

Most infantryman in the Union army carried one form or another of single shot muzzle-loading longarms that fired a paper cartridge, although some metallic cartridge breechloaders, such as the Spencer Rifle, were issued on a limited basis. (USAMHI)

lever-action rifle with its capacity for 16 short copper cased shells. Some Confederates spoke of the last named weapon as "that Damned Yankee rifle that can be loaded on Sunday and fired all week." The backbone of both the Union and Confederate infantry, though, was the rifled .58 caliber musket.

At the outbreak of hostilities tactics did not keep pace with technological improvements in firearms and this conservatism caused considerable pain and death. Increased range and the accuracy of musket fire meant that the days of massed infantry being able to move forward to close in hand-to-hand combat with fixed bayonets were gone forever. One study indicated that of the more than 250,000 Union wounded, most had been brought down by artillery or small arms fire. Only 922 were treated for injuries from bayonets or other edged weapons. Of these, many were the result of self-inflicted actions or accidents, or were a result of confrontations between comrades, mostly while encamped.

Of course there were many instances where bayonet attacks did take place, but their effectiveness seldom, if ever, proved crucial. Nonetheless, clinging to the tradition that the bayonet was a major factor in battle, officers in most units insisted that their commands practice bayonet drill in case they were wielded in combat. In that situation, the troops would be ordered forward without primers in place to prevent them from firing their weapons rather than pressing forward the assault with naked steel. The bayonet also impeded loading – a soldier might impale himself as he rammed home his round.

S. M. Thompson, an infantryman from New Hampshire, chronicled one such bayonet exercise session conducted by his whole brigade. When observed from afar, the gyrating figures looked "like a line of beings made up about equally of the frog, the sand-hill crane, the sentinel crab, and the grasshopper; all of them rapidly jumping, thrusting, swinging, striking, jerking every way, and all gone stark mad."

Routine and pastimes

Every moment, however, was not filled with martial preparations. There were often long lulls in activity some of which were dedicated to housekeeping. Doing laundry, mending clothes, preparing meals, fetching water, and securing fuel for fires were among the tedious, but necessary chores of the common infantryman. Officers might pay an enlisted man to perform these jobs, or hire servants. Even some of the enlisted men employed help for these purposes.

Regardless of whether they had to provide for themselves or had someone to look after their basic requirements, Union infantrymen might be able to enjoy some diversions. Many units had bands that

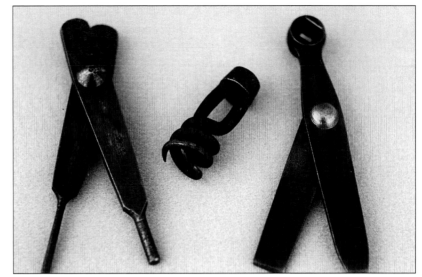

Left to right: combination punch and vent pick, wiper, and M1842 combination screwdriver/cone wrench, all of which were typical accessories used to maintain Union infantry muskets. (WR)

A canister of fulminate of mercury percussion caps. These caps were the most common means of igniting the powder charge to fire a Union musket. The Maynard tape system, a more sophisticated means of priming muzzle-loaders, existed but was considered unreliable and therefore not used to any great extent. (WR)

played for the entertainment of the troops. Some individuals brought their own instruments, and either performed for their own amusement or that of others. Singing was common as well, either solo or as a group activity. The repertoire ranged from popular contemporary tunes to patriotic airs.

Pets were kept, too. Dogs were the most usual choice, but one chap boasted of a squirrel that he carried with him on campaign "through thick and thin" for more than a thousand miles. The little fellow, who was called Bun, supposedly ate "hard-tack like a veteran". Another soldier had settled on a more unlikely animal companion, a Cumberland bear. A third man maintained an owl he had acquired in Arkansas, which he dubbed Minerva. Arguably the most famous of all the critters that would accompany Billy Yank was the bald eagle mascot of the 8th Wisconsin Volunteer Infantry, who shared the honor of bearing Lincoln's nickname, "Old Abe".

Robert W. Patrick mentioned other diversions. During one summer his unit and others bathed in "the clear waters of the placid stream" that ran by their encampment. On land the men pitched quoits (horse-shoes), ran races, jumped, wrestled, or occupied themselves in other physical activities. Perhaps some even played baseball, a relatively new game that was gaining popularity.

Not everyone turned to such lively pursuits, as Patrick further noted: "Hundreds might be seen seated in the shadows of their tents, engaged in reading, or in studies of various kinds in accordance with their tastes and opportunities. Others seemed to spend a great portion of their time in correspondence, shedding ink, as profusely as they had recently shed blood; while many others seemed satisfied, with the mere enjoyment of life, lying for hours on their backs in the warm bath of the sunshine."

Food

Those who were accustomed to having their meals prepared were very disappointed to learn that they had to cook their own food, an experience that was foreign to the majority of the new soldiers. As units assembled, kettles and cooking utensils were distributed to the companies. An individual might try to fend for himself, or throw in his lot with a half dozen or so comrades to form a mess. While arrangements varied from unit to unit, company messes were not required until March 1863, with two to three men being detailed to serve as cooks. Their abilities, though, widely varied.

Even if someone were practiced in food preparation, the ration while encamped was difficult to convert into an appetizing meal. Regulations called for the Union infantryman to receive 12 oz of bacon or pork, or 20 oz of salt or fresh beef, despairingly christened "salt horse" or "old bull", at least three times per week. Likewise some 15 lb of sugar was to be distributed to every 100 soldiers. This sweetener was commonly combined in one small poke sack with the issue coffee, which came both in the bean and as grounds. Later in the war, 8 gallons of beans were to be divided among every 100 men as were 4 gallons of vinegar, 2 lb of salt, 10 lb of rice or hominy, black pepper, yeast powder, and molasses. In

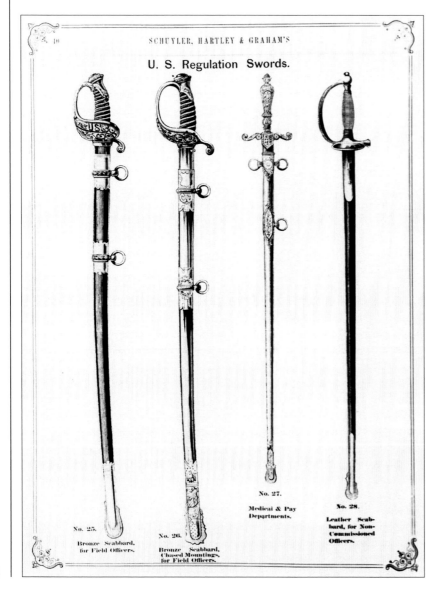

While swords inflicted few casualties in combat, they continued to be carried as badges of office. The two examples on the left were variations available to field grade officers, while the two on the right were for surgeons and paymasters (right center) and certain NCOs starting with first sergeants. (LC)

ABOVE **The utility of bayonets often proved more psychological than practical, but many Union infantrymen still practiced their employment as shown here by men of the 40th Massachusetts Volunteer Infantry. (LC B818-10005)**

RIGHT **It appears this private with the 31st Pennsylvania Volunteer Infantry has managed to bring along his entire family to carry on housekeeping, albeit in a rudimentary fashion. The clothes basket seems to indicate that the woman is a laundress, authorized by regulations as one of the few females granted official status in the Union Army including the issue of rations. (LC B8171-2405)**

RIGHT **Another less fortunate foot soldier in his shirt-sleeves does his own washing. Camp chores were many and tedious, and many men neglected to maintain sanitary standards as a result, thereby contributing to the spread of illness. (NA)**

BELOW **The band of the 107th Regiment U.S. Colored Troops in late 1865 at Fort Cochran, part of the defenses of Washington, DC. (LC B8171-7861)**

Members of the Irish Brigade worship in camp.
(LC B8184-4132)

whatever form obtained, coffee became a central part of the diet. One man recollected it typically was served "strong enough to float an iron wedge".

Twenty-two ounces of bread or flour was allotted daily per man or, when not available (which often proved the case), 16 oz of saltless biscuit made from baked flour and water. Measuring approximately 3 sq. in. and ⅜ in. thick, it was known as pilot's bread since it had been used aboard ship for years. Others called it a cracker or referred to it as hardtack. Regardless of the name, it was not popular, as evidenced by a bit of doggerel from the period that complained:

> "The soldier's fare is very rough,
> The bread is hard, the beef is tough.
> If they can stand it, it will be
> Through love of God, a mystery."

By 1864 a further 6 oz of flour and 4 oz of hardtack were added. Soaking this almost bricklike food in water helped render it slightly more chewable, especially if it was broken up with a rifle butt beforehand. This concoction was dubbed "hellfire stew". When fried in pork fat and water the delectable treat became "skillgalee". For those with more refined tastes, pulverized hardtack could be boiled with salt pork and whatever ingredients might be had to produce a sort of stew

29

the men called "lobscouse". Transforming these crackers into something less than teeth cracking tiles was merely one problem. After being baked, packed in crates, and shipped, this foodstuff might be in the supply system for some time, thereby inviting infestation by less fastidious diners. During the summer of 1864, for example, while engaged in the siege of Petersburg, Chaplain H. Clay Trumbal of the 10th Connecticut Volunteer Infantry reported that his regiment received "wormy" hardtack. After many days of these unsavory victuals, the men grew ill tempered and began to throw away the infested food in their trenches despite orders to keep the area clean. An officer from the brigade eventually noticed this situation. He loudly ordered the offenders to clean up the scraps bellowing, "Don't you know you've no business to throw away hardtack? Haven't you been told that often enough?" One of the soldiers could not resist retorting: "We've thrown it out two or three times sir, but it crawls back."

In other instances the men might not have been so particular about their fare, especially when rations ran low. Even on festive occasions ample staples, much less traditional holiday meals, might not be available. During Christmas 1863 the 6th Iowa Infantry had none of the roast goose, stuffing, or other items so often associated with Yuletide repasts. Instead this unit, along with all the others in their brigade, ate mule soup in a damp, foggy Alabama swamp. The man who "had a hardtack, a piece of raw bacon, and a cup of hot coffee, supplemented with a plug of store tobacco" was considered a fortunate possessor "of rare luxuries" in that "cheerless and uninviting" spot.

ABOVE **The food issued by the government was monotonous and sometimes in short supply. However on special occasions, such as Thanksgiving, a traditional feast might be prepared as depicted by artist Alfred Waud's November 1861 sketch. (LC USZ62-14105)**

When sufficient quantities of staples were on hand, vegetables tended to be scarce. Originally the 2½ oz of dried beans or peas was deemed acceptable. Not until 1864 was a quarter of a pound of potatoes added to the menu or were other vegetables provided, and then only "when practicable". If the fresh variety was not available a desiccated version was supplied, made from shredded beets, carrots, onions, string beans, and other vegetables which were dried then pressed into sheets. Supposedly these dehydrated bundles could be reconstituted by boiling,

Corporal, 7th New York Militia, April 1861
(see plate commentary for full details)

A

Camp scene, 114th Pennsylvania Volunteers

B

Training of the 1st Minnesota, Fort Snelling, 1861

C

Let the punishment fit the crime

22

21

23

2

7

8

10

8

9

12

13

14

11

15

3

3

3

1

20

6

3

5

4

16

17

18

19

US

E

F

Loading a musket
(see plate commentary for full details)

6th Wisconsin at Antietam, September 17 1862

54th Massachusetts at Fort Wagner, July 18 1863

H

Aftermath of battle

Rank had less meaning when it came to visiting the sutler's store, as seen here when a mixture of officers and enlisted infantrymen gather at this forerunner of the military exchange. (NA)

but the result usually left something to be desired; many soldiers referred to this culinary delight as "desecrated vegetables" or "baled hay". One official report put it mildly when it noted these desiccated substitutes were "very disagreeable to the taste". A member of the 13th New Hampshire Volunteer Infantry phrased it another way. In 1863 the desiccated vegetables served the regiment were "dirty, sandy, moldy, and utterly uneatable. The men received them on their plates in liberal quantities and after one taste threw them away in disgust, not caring where they fell – the camp was paved with them.

Officers were inclined to dine better than their subordinates. They were not issued rations, but were given an allowance with which they could buy their food. They also had the latitude to hire enlisted men, sometimes known as "strikers", or they could employ civilians to provide meals and undertake other chores.

Several officers might pool their resources and set up a relatively respectable mess. Some elected, when opportunity allowed, to dine at local hotels or other available eateries. When posted to Washington, DC, in 1861, the 7th New York Militia simply took all their meals in some of the better hostelries of that city.

Needless to say, those men who could not take advantage of such circumstances longed for variety and better provisions. John D. Billings, in his classic memoir, *Hardtack and Coffee*, noted that some relief came from packages sent to the soldier from home. A parcel from loved ones might contain "pudding, turkey, pickles, onions, pepper, paper, envelopes, stockings, potatoes, chocolate, condensed milk [a relatively new item since its introduction in 1856 by Gail Borden], sugar, broma, butter, sauce," and whatever other treasures might be enclosed. Sheldon Colton's brother Carlos, another Union infantry volunteer, even enjoyed receiving "a lot of popcorn with a patent 'wire popper' sent by the family."

LEFT The menu was often far from appetizing. Here Yankee troops fall in for soup. (LC USZ62-3116)

There was another means to supplement the monotonous, meager offerings from Uncle Sam's commissary. Every major headquarter and regiment was authorized a sutler, who provided an array of articles, often at high prices. Tobacco, canned commodities, writing and reading materials, sweets, fruit, and other goods might be had if one possessed the funds to purchase these things. There were even pies and cakes, a provision that was wryly changed to "pi-zan cakes" by troops. Certain medical officers shared the low opinion of these treats, maintaining that the crusts were made of cardboard and the fillings of who knows what.

Some civilian organizations, such as the Union League of Philadelphia, attempted to address the problem of poor diet. These well-meaning efforts had some impact, but soldiers regularly experienced malnutrition, stomach disorders, dysentery, and diarrhea. In fact, wretched nourishment, combined with improper sanitation, and diseases such as measles and malaria, caused more casualties than enemy shot and shell. The rate of sickness averaged 161 men per 1,000 in the Western armies, and 76 per 1,000 in the Eastern armies, the difference in numbers being attributed by Union medical observers of the period to poor nourishment and "the great disposition on the part of the soldiers [in the West] to neglect appliances for personal comfort; and to the greater neglect of, or lack of means for enforcing cleanliness of person and camp." The result was that out of the approximately 300,000 recorded deaths in the Union Army, 42 men out of every 1,000 in Regular Army regiments and 59 men per 1,000 in the volunteer regiments perished of disease. Overall, an estimated one in every nine men in the Federal force died in service. In the final analysis of the Yankees who never returned home, 183,287 succumbed to disease, against 61,362 killed in action and another 34,773 who died of wounds.

Crime, vice and punishment

Bad food, rough conditions, fear, illness, pain, threat of death, and other factors made life precarious for the average soldier, whether in camp or on campaign. One interesting example was the 13th Maine Volunteer Infantry whose Quaker colonel, Neal Dow, accepted "no card playing, swearing drinking, or boisterous" fellows thereby prompting a Boston newspaper to report the 13th was "the quietest regiment that has ever been in seen in this city!"

This was a rather extreme circumstance, however, for many other units and individuals did not display such upright traits. Some sought out prostitutes, gambled, drank to excess, brawled, or became thieves. There also were those who turned to violent crimes.

In a very few situations troops even verged on mutiny. Volunteers unused to strict discipline might revolt against officers, particularly those they thought to be martinets or incompetent. Mutineers in the 79th New York, composed of many men of Scottish descent, and which bore staggering casualties at the First Battle of Bull Run, fell into this category. The matter was dealt with quickly, however. The crux of their revolt was the mandate to set aside their tartans for kersey trousers. The affair was initially handled by negotiation, and the men agreed to return to duty – although the threat of being fired upon by Regular Army infantrymen, and having cannon loaded with cannister leveled at them, was also used to persuade them of the error of their ways. In another incident, German soldiers serving under Maj. Gen. John Frémont threatened to cease their service if their commander was relieved from his post.

Being absent without leave was much more routine. In his diary, Bingham Jankin, who subsequently became a member of the 100th Pennsylvania Volunteer Infantry, reflected that just three days after reporting for duty he "Took french leave and went to Pittsburgh on the morning train; ran around some to see the sights a while ... took dinner; and spent an hour or two there and returned to camp."

One foreign observer thought that more than 30 percent of the troops in some units abused their leaves or passes. Certainly, Maj. Gen. George McClellan informed the president during mid-July 1862 that 40,000 of his Army of the Potomac were absent, and of those 50 percent were fit for duty and had no excuse for being gone. It is unclear how many of these men may have been on some sort of detached duty, another cause that tended to reduce unit strengths.

Desertion posed an even more critical difficulty for Union commanders. During the war some 201,397 cases were reported, with half of those taking place prior to May 1 1863. After that date, heightened efforts to locate absentees helped stem the tide and led to the return of 75,909 men to their outfits. Interestingly, desertion was the highest in Regular Army regiments where 244 men deserted for every 1,000, in contrast to 62 men per 1,000 in the volunteers. These figures do not include the 170,000 who failed to report after receiving their draft notices.

Some of those who fled service did so with the encouragement of family and friends. The war became unpopular with many, and many felt justified in quitting or avoiding service. Another motive for leaving

Pvt. Benjamin Dutcher of the 55th Massachusetts Volunteer Infantry pays for his crime of stealing money from a wounded comrade. (LC B1878-89)

stemmed from greed. With virtually no means of tracking an individual, the practice of offering a man a cash bonus for enlistment caused some money-hungry types to desert from one unit only to show up again elsewhere to claim the cash for joining yet another outfit. These so-called "bounty-jumpers" frustrated military officials. One practitioner confessed to no fewer than 32 desertions until he finally was found out. His sentence for his various misdeeds was four years imprisonment. Diverse punitive measures existed for those convicted of this crime. A member of the 63rd Pennsylvania Infantry received a traditional penalty whereby he was paraded in front of the regiment, his uniform buttons were cut off, his head shaved, and each hip branded with a "D". After this painful marking, he was drummed out of camp wearing a sign made from a hardtack box lid that bore the word "Deserter". Eight men with fixed bayonets escorted him away while the band played "The Rogue's March". As a finale, the assembled troops threw old shoes, tin pans, and whatever else was handy at him as he departed their company forever.

Nearly 300 Union soldiers were executed for murder or desertion during the war. Some faced firing squads. Others, such as Pvt. William Johnson, were hung, as seen here on Jordon's farm near Petersburg, Virginia, in June 1864. (LC B8172-2136

In other situations, desertion and cowardice were dealt with even more summarily. A total of 276 criminals convicted of murder or desertion were executed. A diary account from a man in the 5th Ohio Infantry captured one ghastly form of paying the ultimate penalty for such misdeeds. At 11 am the regiment fell in to hear the orders read, "informing them that between 12 noon and 4 p.m. 3 Deserters would be shot to death by Musketry."

By midday the entire XII Corps formed to witness the affair. An army wagon pulled up in advance bearing a trio of coffins, followed by "an ambulance carrying the three condemned men themselves, with their hands pinioned behind them. Then followed the shooting party from the 46th Regt. P.V. [Pennsylvania Volunteers] numbering about 30 men." Once the coffins had arrived they were removed and placed in front of previously dug graves. The prisoners were blindfolded, marched to their coffins, where they were seated. The provost marshal read the sentence, with the chaplain asking for "mercy on the souls of prisoners. After he stepped back the shooting party came to the ready and in a few more moments a Volley of Musketry insured that the law had been appeased."

At another firing squad, a man who had deserted several times from the 5th New Hampshire Infantry shook hands with his executioners and urged onlookers to "be true to the oath which you have taken, and you will feel better in your own heart. It is only since I received my sentence that I have realized the full enormity of my errors; you should do so whilst you have yet time." Most probably these final words made an indelible impact on those who heard them.

For the most part, however, men were spared this fate because Lincoln pardoned the majority of deserters.

"LAST FULL MEASURE": ON CAMPAIGN

Even if an individual had not witnessed such a chilling incident, he might question whether he had the mettle to stand up to fire. For many it was not fear of death or the pain of wounds, that made them apprehensive, because honor could be earned through these. What worried hundreds and thousands was that they might show "the white feather". Men tended to enlist from their own communities and were surrounded by neighbors and others who knew them, so such a possibility would be horrifying, as word of cowardice would reach home to the humiliation of family and friends. A soldier with the 14th Ohio Volunteer Infantry confessed what it was like at this point when he sent a letter to his wife. He confided, "If I was to turn back now, many would say I was a coward. I would rather be shot at once than to have such a stigma rest on me."

"Just Before the Battle Mother"

Time and again, the Union infantryman had come to grips with this when the decision to engage had been reached. After the lull of winter encampments had ended, preparations would take place to move out in search of the enemy.

One indication of an impending fight might be the issue of three days' worth of field rations, followed by the distribution of 40 to 60 rounds of ammunition. Some of the would-be combatants gobbled up the food, preferring to go into battle with a full stomach and lighter load. There were also some who tossed away spare ammunition to avoid carrying extra weight, a practice which could have dire consequences. In contrast, experienced troops carefully disposed of extraneous material, but made certain they retained the necessities to carry them through the upcoming clash, which would start hours before sunrise with "The Long Roll" being sounded.

The commanding officer might address the troops at this point, as did a major with the 13th New Hampshire Volunteer Infantry, who made this short speech: "You love your country, you are brave men, and you have come here to fight for her. Now go Forward!"

At Chancellorsville Col. Robert Riley made a brief appeal to the men of his 75th Ohio Volunteer Infantry. He acknowledged: "some of you will not see another sunrise." With that he offered, "If any man in the ranks is not ready to die for his country, let him come to me and I will give him a pass to go to the rear, for I want no half-hearted, unwilling soldiers or cowards in the ranks." None asked for this relief, and so they went to confront the supreme test. Many died that day, including their colonel.

Once the speeches had been made and the preparations completed, the troops were given the order to move out. Union infantryman Leverett Holden rendered a January 1863 version of this ritual: "We had reveille [wake-up call on bugle, drum, or fife] early the next morning, and in the midst of a nasty, cold, and penetrating rain storm started again on the same road we had marched over the previous day. The men were in mighty ill humor, cold, wet, and dirty; but moved according to orders, all thoroughly of the opinion that the march, and the battle, in prospective, must prove disastrous."

In fact, contact with the enemy's main body never took place. The men turned around as Holden narrated from their "never-to-be-forgotten, dirty miserable trip." They had not lost "any men killed or wounded; but the army returned to camp, after being away some four days, disaffected and dissatisfied, with a mighty poor opinion of their commanding officer."

During the summer of 1861 the 21st Illinois Volunteer Infantry experienced a similar situation. Their colonel, a West Point graduate and veteran of the Mexican War, was apprehensive as he rode in the lead of his unit to meet with the Confederates under Col. Thomas Harris, whose command was reported to be located near a town about 25 miles march away. Passing through the deserted countryside, the 21st finally came to "the brow of a hill from which it was expected we could see Harris' camp, and possibly find his men ready formed to meet us." The Union colonel found his "heart kept getting higher and higher until it felt to me it was in my throat. I would have given anything then to have been back in Illinois, but I had not the moral courage to halt and consider what to do. I kept right on."

Then, when the 21st reached their destination they looked into the valley where they expected to spy the enemy. "The place where Harris had been encamped a few days before was still there … but the troops were gone. My heart resumed its place. It occurred to me at once that Harris had been as much afraid of me as I had been of him." The reluctant colonel was Ulysses S. Grant, the man destined to head the Union Army in the last stages of the war.

Cpl. Charlie Maguda was one of over 180,000 African Americans who served in the Union Army, for the most part as foot soldiers. (GNMP)

Representative engagements

Not every incident came to such an end. Typically, the enemy was encountered and a struggle ensued. The personal nature of the conflict was one of its most poignant features as illustrated by an incident that took place at Malvern Hill (July 1 1862). The Irish Brigade found itself in the fray, as it would many times during the war. Confederate forces had pinned down one of the brigade's companies under Capt. D. P. Conyngham.

A sergeant who numbered among the best shots in the brigade was called upon to help dislodge the enemy. Having observed the young Rebel lieutenant in front of his men rallying them on as they kept up steady fire from an adjacent wood, Conyngham called out to the sharpshooting Sergeant Driscoll, "If that officer is not taken down, many of us will fall before we pass that clump" of trees. Driscoll acknowledged his captain, brought his rifle up, aimed, and fired. The officer went down, and the Confederates broke and ran.

As Conyngham's troops moved up, he told Driscoll to "See if that officer is dead – he was a brave fellow." The sergeant obeyed, and as he turned over the man he had just killed, Conyngham heard the dying Confederate utter, "Father", then he closed his eyes forever. Driscoll's round had killed his own son.

Unable to halt in the midst of this tragedy, the captain's company was told to close with the foe. Obediently his men moved forward. In time Sergeant Driscoll took the lead and yelled to his comrades to follow him. Conyngham reported that the sergeant "soon fell, but jumped up again. We knew he was wounded. On he dashed, but he soon rolled over like a top. When we came up he was dead, riddled with bullets."

Although this sad case would not be repeated in the brigade's history, the unit was not spared further misery. By September 17 1862 it was again on the move. This time the "boyos" were heading toward a sunken wagon road in the vicinity of Antietam, Maryland. By day's end the tiny, rutted road would receive an appropriate name: "Bloody Lane".

The sons of Eire moved to support Brig. Gen. William French's command, who earlier in the engagement had come into contact with deadly Southern riflemen. Previously French's first wave had halted to dress their lines as a small band struck up a tune.

Observing their movements from behind rail fences across the sunken road, the Confederate commander, Col. John Gordon, watched in awe. "The men in blue … formed in my front," and those in the first row came to the position of "charge bayonet" while the rest brought their weapons to "right shoulder arms". To Gordon, the Yankee preparations were "a thrilling spectacle" causing him to lament "what a pity to destroy with bullets such a scene of martial beauty." Despite such regrets, the colonel gave the command to fire. Gordon saw the entire Union "front line" topple "in the consuming blast" from his men.

On the receiving end, Thomas Galway of the 8th Ohio Infantry, another regiment taking part in the fight (not as part of the Irish Brigade), tersely captured the moment. He said, "The din was frightful. Nothing could describe it." Galway only could liken it to "systematic killing". He was correct, because within five minutes some 410 Union infantrymen had been put out of action, while the Confederate defenders remained virtually untouched. A decade and a half before the

Charles Springer was the sergeant-major of the 107th U.S. Colored Troops. His rank is indicated by chevrons made of sky-blue silk tape with three arcs above three stripes, in accordance with regulations of the era. (GNMP)

The 9th New York Volunteers (also known as Hawkins' Zouaves, Little Zouaves, and Zoo-Zoos) styled themselves after French zouaves complete with red fezzes for the enlisted men. (NA)

war, Union officer Henry Halleck had asserted in his *Elements of Military Art and Science* that one entrenched infantryman was equal to a half-dozen attackers. At that moment it appeared his thesis was correct.

Union leaders now called upon the Irish Brigade to enter the maelstrom. As Charles Hall moved forward with his unit, he observed a woman who had accompanied her husband on the campaign cheering on her spouse with indifference to the raging battle. This stiffened Hall's determination, as perhaps to a Catholic chaplain it did. Appearing in front of the moving ranks on horseback, the priest rode down the line blessing the men and dispensing absolution. This was most appropriate because many of the brigade were about to meet their maker. By way of example, half of the 63rd New York would be struck down as they marched into the fray.

Yet the Irish continued to push toward their adversary. In the opening march their smoothbore .69 caliber muskets had limited effect, but as they closed the distance their "buck and ball" rounds (one large lead slug and three smaller ones) began to even the score. Still victory was not at hand. Ammunition began to run low before they had completed their bold tramp to Bloody Lane. The living had to gather cartridges from the dead to sustain the fight.

More and more of their number fell, including Capt. Patrick Clooney. Although wounded, the plucky Irishman regained his feet and picked up a toppled flag from its bearer, who had been struck. He trudged ahead as did others, eventually driving the Confederates from their defense. Sheer audacity in the face of deadly marksmanship had brought them to this point.

As the survivors reached the former enemy stronghold, Charles Hall spied a badly wounded Rebel who called out, "Say, Yank, for the love of

God," move the dead body lying across "my legs." Hall did, and then pressed on. He was one of the fortunate ones.

When the din ceased and the smoke cleared, between 23,000 and 29,000 Northerners and Southerners had been hit. The Irish Brigade's 69th New York alone had sustained a 60 percent loss. During the 11 hours of hell, a man was killed or wounded every two seconds. This had been the bloodiest day of the war, but the carnage did not stop there.

Two years later, this time near Petersburg, Virginia, another confrontation was recorded, in short bursts by the adjutant of the 3rd Delaware Volunteer Infantry: "Down we lay on a field the shells whizzing over and around us. Up rides an aid[e] to [the] brigade commander whispers with a few words & dashes away. Attention 3d Brigade. Forward and away we go, come to the briars, go through head long over stumps, bushs [sic] & all not in a nice line of battle but like a big flock of stray sheep – officers shouting, men halloing [sic] & growling. 'Swing up that left back on right. Keep by those colors. Hold on … two men are enough to carry that man, steady men['] and so we go till we reach the edge of the woods. 'Halt! Officers form your companies!' Again we form a decent line. 'Fix bayonets.' *We* know what that means. 'Forward!' 'Yell boys' Yeh! Yeh-Yeh! Double quick and away we go shouting as loud as we can and, you may not believe it, but cheering is half the battle when we charge."

Aftermath

When the rush of combat subsided the participants experienced a range of emotions and situations. Sometimes after an engagement the atmosphere might be relaxed or even have some comical moments, as set forth in the recollections of an infantryman with the Army of the Potomac. During a lull in hostilities at Spotsylvania, Frank Wilkeson volunteered to fetch water for his unit. When he arrived at a nearby spring he came upon many "hallow-eyed, tired looking men … but not 'coffee boilers,' lying on the ground sleeping soundly." There was one exception. Wilkeson spied a blond, bewhiskered colonel of infantry who "looked around quickly; his face hardened with resolution." With that the officer "took a cartridge out of his vest pocket, tore the paper with his strong white teeth, spilled the powder into his right palm, spat on it, then, first casting a quick glance around to see if he was observed, he rubbed the moistened powder on his face and hands." To complete his appearance the colonel "dust coated the war paint" and was instantly "transformed from a trembling coward who lurked behind a tree into an exhausted brave taking a little well-earned repose."

There were many who did not have to resort to such measures to pretend they had become warriors. Reflecting on the repulsed attack on Fort Wagner, along the coast of South Carolina in July 1863, the sergeant-major of the 54th Massachusetts Volunteer Infantry wrote: "The battle is over. It is midnight. The ocean beach is crowded with the dead, the dying, and the wounded. It is with difficulty that you can urge your horse through the sands. Faint lights are glimmering in the sand holes, and rifle pits as you pass down the beach. In these holes many a poor soldier wounded and bleeding has laid down to his last sleep." In the face of this suffering and desolation the sergeant-major managed to tell his intended, "Remember, if I die, I die in a good cause."

Voluntary Assisting the wounded on the field of Battle

OPPOSITE, TOP **A dressing station in operation after the devastating carnage of Antietam. (LC USZ62-1059)**

OPPOSITE, BELOW **After Antietam these Yankee zouaves practice ambulance drill with mock casualties. (LC B8171-7381)**

RIGHT **Wounded Billy Yanks at a makeshift hospital set up following the Wilderness campaign. (LC B8184-740)**

BELOW **Some 20,000 American Indians served on both sides during the Civil War, including these infantry sharpshooters who were wounded at Marye's Heights near Fredericksburg, Maryland. (LC B811-2342)**

Sheldon Colton was one of those who faced wounding and possible death. At the battle of Kernstown, command of Company K fell to the young subaltern, who moved forward with his men. Drawing his revolver Colton came to a rail fence and leaned forward slightly to see if his revolver would reach the enemy from where he had halted. Before he could discharge a round, "a ball struck the pair of scissors" he carried in "his vest pocket breaking one point and bending the other." Some of the force of the shot had been deflected by these implements and Colton's

A wounded zouave with his .58 caliber musket resting next to him is looked after by a Union foot soldier wearing the standard sky-blue kersey overcoat and a forage cap that has the added protection of a detachable rain cover. The scene no doubt was staged because the men are in a winter camp. During this season fighting was all but suspended. (NA)

pocket diary. Nonetheless, the bullet "glanced down" penetrating his body "about two inches forward of the joint of the hip bone, passing through the bone in a semicircular direction, grazing as it went along and lodging about two inches around the joint of the bone."

The injured officer was operated on the next day, and the ball removed. After that, the wound kept running constantly, but a local Quaker woman took him in and tended the patient, who wrote to his mother that his injury did not cause him much pain. Months later, he still was required to dress his incision because it still had not healed completely. He would have to be discharged as no longer being fit for combat duty. Colton ultimately regained his health, and in this regard was more fortunate than many who had lost a limb, eyesight, or their life.

Badges of courage

Some of those who had been severely or mortally wounded would be among those who were recognized in a special way. In July 1862 President Lincoln approved the Medal of Honor for those soldiers and (as of March 3 1863 those officers) who displayed gallantry in action. In the more than 1,000 engagements fought during the War of the Rebellion, some 1,200 men, most of whom were infantrymen, would be

By spring 1865 most Union infantrymen who had managed to survive the war could stack their muskets and return home. (LC B8171-3229)

singled out to receive this decoration. While medals had long been regarded as the trappings of foreign military establishments, this decoration was accepted and ultimately gained prestige.

The deeds for which the Medal of Honor were presented varied. Many times the capturing of the enemy flag or saving a unit's colors was the reason for bestowing the medal. Other times it might be given for saving the lives of comrades, such as in the case of 12-year-old drummer boy Willie Johnston of Company D, 3rd Vermont Volunteer Infantry. This youngest recipient of the Medal of Honor rescued his commanding officer, while Chaplain Francis Hall of the 19th New York Volunteer Infantry carried wounded from the field under fire.

At Vicksburg, a sergeant from Company D, 99th Illinois Volunteer Infantry, Thomas J. Higgins, forged ahead even after his regiment had fallen back, having been repulsed during a failed assault. Determined to advance, Higgins kept moving toward the Rebel lines. When he reached them, the sergeant planted the flag on the enemy parapet, and was captured. Over three decades later, the Medal of Honor was conferred upon him because veterans of the 2nd Texas, his former foes who had watched him with admiration that day, urged federal authorities to acknowledge the bravery of this man.

"With malice toward none"

Putting aside old hatred was uppermost in Lincoln's mind as the conflict drew to a close. The quick, easy victory envisioned at the beginning of the war had proved an illusion. Rather than lasting a few months, the contest raged for four bloody years. In the end, the North triumphed. The long-suffering, hard-fighting Yankee infantrymen from farmsteads, hamlets, and urban centers had helped save the Union.

HALLOWED GROUND

Sheldon Colton left the 67th Ohio and returned to civilian life after the war, while John "Johnny Shiloh" Clem continued in service until 1913, when he retired as a major-general, and the last active-duty service veteran of the Civil War. Most followed Colton's course, but even after returning to their homes and families, few forgot the experience. One of their numbers, a Yankee foot soldier from Iowa, spoke for many when he wrote: "War is hell broke loose, and makes men brutes, yet I would not have missed this for any consideration."

These former soldiers formed an organization known as the Grand Army of the Republic. They marched in parades, held meetings of their local chapters, and met with affiliates from other branches of the "GAR" at regional or national encampments that allowed the seasoned campaigners to gather with old comrades and relive the days of their youth. They became a powerful political force for decades to come, and in fact nearly every president from U. S. Grant to William McKinley had served under the Union banner.

Moreover, the federal government published the *Official Record of the War of the Rebellion*, besides an outpouring of unit histories, and a flood of individual memoirs, all of which kept the flame of memory bright. This national drama had touched almost every family North and South.

Lest the country forget, monuments were erected on village greens or at the places where Billy Yank had faced Johnny Reb. A number of these former killing fields were set aside as hallowed ground. Some, such as the cemetery at Gettysburg, had been consecrated even as the war raged. Little wonder, then, that not long after the fighting ended,

There were considerable lulls in fighting, especially during winter when soldiers might have time to work on crafts, such as this homemade pipe bowl. It is carved from mountain laurel with a hollowed shrub twig stem, held to a bone mouth piece by a surplus oiler top, and has a silver inkwell for a lid. The head wears a typical forage cap. (WR)

reunions began to reunite veterans, sometimes from both sides, at many of the places that had been baptized by their blood. But it was not just the combatants that made pilgrimages to these sites.

Battlefields and museums

In the many years since the cessation of hostilities, millions of visitors have trekked to Civil War sites, from Fort Sumter on the eastern seaboard, to Drum Barracks on the west coast, and other places at nearly every point of the compass, including Ship Island in the balmy Gulf of Mexico, or Fort Snelling in the northern climes of Minnesota.

The National Park Service, an agency of the United States Department of the Interior, has been charged with the preservation of many of these sites, but state and local governments, along with some private groups and individuals operate sites and museums around the country. Published guides list many of them. Additionally, many are listed on the internet. Among the most useful addresses are:

> www.civil-war.net
> www.civilwar.org
> www.historychannel.com
> www.sunsite.ktu.edu/civil-war

These contain links to many parks, battlefields, historic sites, and museums that are available to the public. Certain associations, most notably the Civil War Preservation Trust (which can be found at www.civilwar.org), work to promote the preservation and interpretation of these links with a bygone era.

Re-enactors

American Civil War re-enacting grew in popularity during the centennial of the War of the Rebellion and has remained strong in the United States, with a considerable following in Europe. Additionally, for a brief period a glossy magazine dedicated to re-enacting of all eras was published. While this short-lived periodical has been discontinued, *The Camp Chase Gazette*, *North-South Trader*, and *Smoke & Fire News* offer coverage of local, regional, and national events. Also of use are *Civil War Times Illustrated*, *America's Civil War*, and *North and South*. For those interested in becoming a participant in living history of this period, R. Lee Hadden's *Reliving the Civil War* furnishes a solid foundation, while Alan Wellikoff's *Civil War Supply Catalogue* gives some idea of the range of replica items that can be obtained today.

Collecting

Everything from spent musket balls to ornate presentation swords have long been considered desirable by collectors. Dealers advertise in firearms magazines, and periodicals such as *Military History*. Auction houses and on-line auctions list collectibles for bid. There are collectors' shows at many places including Baltimore, Maryland, Chantilly, Virginia, and Gettysburg. At Gettysburg many shops are open to the public, selling a wide array of artifacts, limited edition prints, and reproduction items. Certain other historic sites also have military or antique stores in the vicinity that handle items of interest. Because many Civil War pieces fetch high prices, fakes and forgeries abound. Even experts can be fooled. Certainly the watchwords are "let the buyer beware".

The legacy

A bibliophile could spend a fortune acquiring books, pamphlets, and periodicals treating almost every conceivable aspect of the war. Hollywood has certainly done its share to spark interest, although seldom with anything approaching accuracy. More recently, the information explosion generated by the internet, home video, and cable channels has added further fuel to the passionate pursuit of this compelling era, which to borrow from Lincoln's first inaugural address has seemingly touched "The mystic chords of memory, stretching from every battlefield, and patriot grave, to every living heart and hearthstone" in the land. In many respects this long, widespread affinity to a tragic yet noble conflict rests on the sacrifices of those Union infantrymen who helped reforge a nation torn asunder by four costly years of civil war.

A number of Civil War collectibles exist, such as this handsome pair of epaulets for a captain of infantry in their japanned tin metal carrying case. Such finery was usually put aside for the duration of the war. (WR)

BIBLIOGRAPHY

Billings, John D., *Hardtack and Coffee, or the Unwritten Story of Army Life,* Boston, 1888.

Boatner, Mark M. III, *The Civil War Dictionary,* New York, 1959.

Botkin, B. A., *A Civil War Treasury of Tales, Legends & Folklore,* New York, 1993.

Eicher, David J., *Civil War Battlefields: A Touring Guide,* Dallas, 1995.

Gates, Betsey, *The Colton Letters: Civil War Period,* Scottsdale, 1993.

Griffith, Paddy, *Battle Tactics of the Civil War,* New Haven, 1989.

Groene, Bertham H., *Tracing Your Civil War Ancestor,* New York, 1973.

Hadden, R. Lee, *Reliving the Civil War: A Reenactor's Handbook,* Mechanicsburg, PA, 1999.

Livermore, Thomas L., *Numbers and Losses in the Civil War in America,* Boston, 1901.

Lord, Francis A., *They Fought for the Union,* New York, 1960.

Ostrander, Alson B., *An Army Boy of the Sixties,* Yonkers, 1924.

Pohanka, Brian C., *Don Troiani's Civil War,* Mechanicsburg, PA, 1995.

Railsback, Thomas C., and Langellier, John P., *The Drums Would Roll: A Pictorial History of US Army Bands on the American Frontier, 1866-1900,* London, 1987.

Robertson, James L., Jr., *Soldiers Blue & Gray,* New York, 1988.

Shively, Julie, *The Ideal Guide to American Civil War Places,* Nashville, 1999.

Wellikoff, Alan, *Civil War Supply Catalogue: A Comprehensive Source Book of Products from the Civil War Era Available Today,* New York, 1996.

Wiley, Bell, *The Life of Billy Yank: The Common Soldier of the Union,* Baton Rouge, 1997.

COLOR PLATE COMMENTARY

A: CORPORAL, 7TH NEW YORK MILITIA, APRIL 1861

At the time of the attack on Fort Sumter the Regular Army had only ten regiments on its rolls. A number of militia units also existed in both the North and South at that time, but few were well trained or equipped. One exception was the 7th New York Militia.

Although originally formed as an artillery unit, the 7th had served as foot soldiers even before the war, mastering the convoluted drill of the period. This proficiency, and their uniforms of gray coatees, black shakos, and white cross belts, caused them to be compared favorably with West Point cadets of the antebellum era.

1. When war erupted they set aside their ornate outfits for a field uniform of short gray jackets and trousers, both of which were trimmed in black. A jaunty gray French-style chasseur forage cap with black band and brass company numeral on the front completed the campaign uniform.

2. They strapped on rigid black waterproofed knapsacks topped with the caped overcoat, when this garment was not required for wear, or their rolled blanket. Regardless of what they placed atop the backpack, this accessory should have been large enough to haul all the soldier's necessities except the footstools provided for each member of the regiment for use in camp.

3. Although various types of knapsacks and backpacks existed during the war, the haversack was always present. Made of black enameled cotton cloth typically measuring about 12.5 in. x 13 in., secured by a leather closure strap, and suspended from a matching shoulder strap, this all-purpose bag had a plain cotton liner buttoned inside. Despite its widespread use, some veterans considered the item "an unwieldy burden" which might contain "stolen truck enough to load a mule" tossed in with "bacon, pork, salt junk, sugar, coffee, tea, desiccated vegetables, rice, bits or yesterday's dinner, and old scraps." Another savvy campaigner noted that after a few weeks "as a receptacle for chunks of fat bacon and fresh meat, damp sugar tied up in a rag," the "odorous haversack" soon "took on the color of a printing office towel. It would have been alike offensive to the eyes and nose of a fastidious person."

4. The daily field ration hauled about in this reeking bag was to consist of 1 lb of hardtack, ¾ lb of salt pork, which often was tainted, or 1¼ lb of fresh meat (**4a**), plus (**4b-d**) salt, sugar, and coffee. Supposedly five days worth of this food could be packed away in this commissary on the hip.

In addition, the haversack was sometimes pressed into service to lug items traditionally kept in knapsacks or backpacks, such as shoes, (**5**) candles and (**6**) holders, (**7**) shaving implements, chewing tobacco or (**8**) cigars, (**9**) a block of "lucifers" (wooden stick matches), (**10**) photographs, (**11**) a "housewife" (sewing kit), (**12**) toiletries, (**13**) Bible, (**14**) toothbrush, (**15**) handkerchiefs, (**16**) underwear, (**17**) a mess plate, and utensils, sometimes ones that were (**18**) combined knife, fork and spoon implements, (**19**) pen, ink, and paper.

20. Tin canteens covered in gray or blue cloth were suspended from a cotton sling and held three pints of water or other liquid. Prior to the war, smooth-sided versions had been issued, but early in the conflict a model with concentric rings came into use which weighed slightly less than its predecessor. A metal reinforced cork held to the pewter throat by a chain and ring kept the contents from spilling. While the majority of men used this item, there were wooden, leather, and other styles of metal canteens that were issued or were available for purchase.

21. Metal collapsible cups or rigid cups of many sizes and shapes were pressed into service by Billy Yank as a combination drinking implement/soup dispenser. Soldiers might fashion "coffee boilers" of various types that were little more than metal cups rigged with a wire to hang over a fire for the purpose of brewing coffee or making soup. Some of these even had pouring spouts and lids. In fact, doughboys might discard their canteens in favor of "a good strong tin cup," claiming "it was easier to fill at a well or spring, and was more serviceable as a boiler for making coffee."

22. The Seventh wore a white buff leather waist belt with stamped brass plate to which the bayonet and bayonet scabbard and the cap pouch were suspended. Ammunition for the M1855 rifle musket in .58 caliber (**23**) was carried in a cartridge box which bore a cast NY on the black leather flap. (**24**) This accoutrement was worn over the shoulder, being suspended by a white buff leather belt.

B: CAMP SCENE, 114TH PENNSYLVANIA VOLUNTEERS

During the antebellum era both Northern and Southern militiamen looked toward Europe for inspiration in weapons, uniforms, accoutrements, and drill. Many units particularly admired France's elite zouaves, and many units mimicked the jaunty attire of these troops who had gained such distinction in the Crimean War. Sometimes the appearance of these militiamen was nearly identical to that of their role models; in other instances, the troops only vaguely resembled Gallic prototypes.

The uniforms of the 114th Pennsylvania Volunteer Infantry Regiment (Collis Zouaves) were fairly faithful to the original H. T. Collis, and the men made a considerable splash when they showed up in their colorful garb as one of the early outfits assigned to the Army of the Potomac. During their winter encampment at Frederick, Maryland, the captain even carried the theme further by dining on omelet soufflés prepared by his enlisted cook. The rank and file did not necessarily enjoy the same treats: here, a 50 lb box of hardtack (known by various unflattering terms such as "sheet iron crackers" or "teeth dullers") has been opened and is ready for distribution, but the tiny group of comrades seems uninterested in it.

By 1862 Collis was charged with raising an entire regiment, which followed the same regulations in terms of its uniform. Unlike many units that first had appeared in such a costume, but eventually abandoned the look, the 114th wore their zouave ensemble to the end of the war. The regiment also boasted a band and a *vivandière* (a sutler), a woman named Mary (or Marie) Tebe. The presence of women in camps differed from unit to unit: sometimes they served as nurses, laundresses, or cooks; in other instances they were simply camp followers.

C: TRAINING OF THE 1ST MINNESOTA, FORT SNELLING, 1861

Most incoming recruits had never served in the military. Even those with a prewar militia background sometimes knew little about the profession of arms. Learning the basics of marching, which was carried on at a prescribed 90 paces (70 yards) per minute in "common time", 110 paces (86 yards) per minute in "quick time", and 140 paces (109 yards) in "double quick time," proved taxing to instructors who found that some of their raw recruits did not know left from right. This meant that pieces of hay and straw were sometimes placed in the new soldier's shoes and the cadence called out "Hay foot, straw foot" by a frustrated NCO or officer. Adding to the problem was the fact that some Yankee foot soldiers did not understand English.

Like so many other Billy Yanks, new inductees of the 1st Minnesota spent their days attempting to become familiar with the ways of a soldier. In June and July of 1861 they gathered at Fort Snelling in their home state to undergo transformation from civilians to soldiers. During this period there was no uniformity within the regiment as to their armament; some companies had received .58 caliber M1855 rifled muskets, while others obtained M1842 rifles or even smoothbores that had been converted from flintlocks.

Their clothes were also a hodgepodge, a common situation during the early phases of the war. One company showed up in gray outfits fashioned by local women. Another group had secured outdated Regular Army uniforms, and yet a third element had donned blue or red woolen shirts and dark blue trousers turned out by a tailor in the area.

In one effort to attain some consistency, patriotic seamstresses made up 600 havelocks. These white cloth cap covers had been named after Henry Havelock, a British general serving in India, who helped popularize this accessory. Some claimed it to be "indispensable to the soldier's comfort", but these gifts proved impractical as combat items and were pressed into service as nightcaps, bandages, and towels.

D: LET THE PUNISHMENT FIT THE CRIME

Discipline is a key to success in the military. Consequently, departure from rules and regulations prompted several forms of penalties in Union infantry units. Thieves, such as the man in the four-button sack coat with non-regulation slouch hat, might have to wear a sign proclaiming their offense. Another soldier carries a heavy log in the hot sun and to add to his sentence wears a sky-blue kersey overcoat with attached cape. A third prisoner has been "bucked and gagged", a punishment whereby the guilty party was restrained in a sitting position with his hands tied under the legs so he could not stand, then a stout stick or bayonet was forced into the mouth and held in place by a rope or cord. Their guard walks his station in the widely used dark blue four-button blouse and sky-blue kersey trousers that ultimately became the most common garb of the Union infantryman.

E: MUZZLE-LOADERS

Union cartridge boxes were available in several models depending on the soldier's weapon. They were usually worn on the right hip at the waist, usually from an over-the-shoulder strap (1), although sometimes they were belt mounted (2). One of the most common types was the M1855 (3, open, rear, side and underneath views shown) made of black harness leather measuring 6.8 in. by 5.2 in. by 1.4 in.,

with a separately attached lead-filled brass oval plate bearing the letters "US". A pair of tin liners (4) were inserted inside to hold 40 .58 caliber paper cartridges (5), half of which were upright, and the other half bundled in packets and placed in the lower portion of the inserts. There also was a small pocket with flap for basic tools used to maintain the weapon (6). In 1864 a nearly identical design was issued, but rather than the brass plate on the outer flap, a "US" within an oval was embossed directly to the leather flap, thereby reducing the expense of making the box. A similar box (7) in a larger size (7.8 in. by 4.7 in. by 1.6 in.) was provided for .69 caliber muskets.

A small pouch (8) positioned forward of the right hip contained the caps (9) that were used to fire the muzzle-loading longarms. These resembled miniature copper top hats and were filled with fulminate of mercury, a substance that when struck by the hammer would spark and ignite the powder into the barrel of the musket. The pouch itself (8) had a larger outer cover held shut by a brass finial. A small inner flap helped keep moisture out, while an interior fleece lining prevented the caps from rattling around. A thin wire vent pick also was inserted inside as a means to unclog a plugged nipple fouled from firing.

Also shown is a typical lock mechanism of a percussion musket (10). When the soldier pulled the trigger the sear pressed up against the tumbler and activated the mainspring, which in turn pulled the tumbler down thereby causing the hammer to drop on the nipple. The .69 caliber smoothbore musket could be fired with a round lead ball of that size (11) or with a ball and three smaller buckshot, known as "buck and ball" (12) with a range of up to 200 yards; the rifled version in this caliber could unleash a lethal Minié bullet (13). In turn, .58 caliber rifled muskets fired either the deadly Minié ball (14) with relative accuracy at 300 yards and could go to 750 yards, or could be loaded with cartridges containing a dozen lead buckshots (15) to provide a wider pattern that was most effective at close range.

16: While there was considerable variation in the field uniform of the Union infantryman the dark blue flannel four-button sack coat, sky-blue kersey trousers, and forage cap was the most common campaign outfit by the war's end. 17: A rear view of a soft knapsack, an article that was not as popular for carrying the soldier's personal items as the haversack. 18: The grey woolen issue bed blanket typically displayed a heavily stitched US in the center and had black broad stripes near each end. 19: Rubberized ponchos provided some protection against rain, but often were discarded by troops in the field. Also shown is a late-war shelter tent (20): it had metal buttons, and commonly measured 5 ft 6 in. x 5 ft 5 in.

21: Triangular bayonets were common and used with such weapons as the M1842 .69 caliber M1842 musket (22). The M1861 .58 caliber rifled musket (23) emerged as the weapon of choice for many Union foot soldiers. It proved lethal in the hands of a trained infantryman.

F: LOADING A MUSKET

An experienced Union infantryman could discharge three rounds per minute. By modern standards this seems slow, but because most Union foot soldiers were armed with muzzle-loading weapons that required several steps to operate, this rate of fire represented an impressive accomplishment. The men were taught to perform this function on command or to operate independently. In either case the process was essentially the same.

E. Benjamin Andrews of the 4th Connecticut Volunteer Infantry recounted that when troops in his unit were still "green" their capabilities were anything but impressive. During their first engagement the inexperienced foot soldiers wondered "Which end of the cartridge shall go downwards? About a third of the men, reasoning apriori [sic] that the bullet was the main thing, put it in first. A good number of those who did not do this failed to tear the paper. Several put two or three cartridges in; some even more."

1: The proper means of firing a muzzle-loading firearm produced a more reliable outcome. First, the infantryman placed his musket between his feet, holding the weapon away from him with the left hand while reaching to the rear with his right hand to open the outer flap of his cartridge box and lift the inner flap to reveal the tin inserts containing the paper cartridges.

2: The cartridge was extracted from the box and raised to the mouth, where the individual used his teeth to tear open the back end of the heavy paper to expose the black gunpowder. One important aspect of the medical exam at the beginning of an enlistment was to ascertain whether the prospective recruit had a sufficiency of good teeth to perform this function.

3: Next, he "charged the cartridge" by pouring the powder down the barrel, and stuffing the paper along with the bullet into the muzzle.

4: At this point he would withdraw the ramrod from the channel under the stock below the barrel and shove the bullet and paper atop the powder to the end of the tube, seating all firmly.

5: The ramrod was removed and returned to its proper place. According to Hardee's manual, only the little finger was to be used to push the rammer back down the stock in case the weapon accidentally fired, in which case the soldier would only lose a small appendage rather than sustain a wound to the whole hand. Sometimes in the heat of battle, however, a soldier could fail to withdraw the ramrod, thereby firing it like a harpoon. He might hit an enemy in this way, but it was unlikely. What was certain under the circumstance is that his weapon was rendered useless unless he could come up with a replacement from a fallen comrade or by another means.

6: If the soldier had replaced the ramrod in its groove, he was ready to "prime" his piece. Placing his musket at half-cock (leaving it on the partially cocked position for safety which meant, theoretically, the weapon could not fire; this is the origin of the term "going off at half-cock", meaning not being ready), he reached for the small pouch at his waist, opened its outer flap and inner flap, and withdrew the percussion cap, which he placed on the musket's nipple below the hammer.

7: Bringing his weapon up to his shoulder, he cocked the hammer and aimed.

8: With the butt firmly in place and the target in his sights, the man could squeeze the trigger; then repeat the process upon command or independently. Usually this was accomplished while standing up because a muzzle-loader was often almost as tall as the man using it, and loading in the prone or kneeling position was awkward at best.

G: 6TH WISCONSIN AT ANTIETAM, SEPTEMBER 17 1862

Early in the war the 6th Wisconsin Infantry, along with the 2nd and 7th Wisconsin, as well as the 19th Indiana, had been placed under the command of Brig. Gen. John Gibbon. The four regiments soon became known as the Black Hat Brigade because of the 1858-pattern regulation hats worn by enlisted men. On August 28 the brigade underwent its baptism of fire, as the Second Bull Run campaign was drawing to a close. The unit sustained 33 percent casualties during that engagement against Stonewall Jackson's wing of the Army of Northern Virginia. Over the next three weeks the men faced the Confederates in five battles, sustaining 58 percent killed and wounded.

By September 17 these hardened veterans were again thrown into the fray, this time at Sharpsburg. By now the 24th Michigan had joined their greatly reduced ranks. On that fateful Wednesday morning, one of the officers of the 6th, Maj. Rufus R. Dawes, recalled how the regiment was drawn up and moved forward through Miller's cornfield. The command "Forward-guide left-march!" was given. The men moved abreast as the Confederates opened fire. When the regiment "appeared at the edge of the corn, a long line of men in butternut and gray rose up from the ground." According to the major, "simultaneously, the hostile battle lines opened fire upon each other." He went on to report, "Men, I can not say fell; they were knocked out of the ranks by the dozens." At this point "There was great hysterical excitement, eagerness to go forward, and a reckless disregard of life, of everything but victory."

When the intense fighting ended, 150 of the 280 men of the regiment had been killed or wounded. Because of this heroic charge by the 6th and its brother regiments the entire unit was given another nickname "the Iron Brigade". Little did these foot soldiers realize that this honor came at a high price. The battle of Antietam would be remembered as the bloodiest single day of the American Civil War.

H: 54TH MASSACHUSETTS AT FORT WAGNER, JULY 18 1863

When Lincoln at last permitted African Americans to be recruited into the Union Army, there were some who questioned whether they would fight. The answer was yes. Men who had been enslaved in the South or treated with scorn in the North would rise to the occasion when called upon to help save a nation that had treated them unjustly.

Nowhere was this more evident than on July 18 1863, when the 54th Massachusetts Volunteer Infantry launched a heroic attack against Fort Wagner, South Carolina. This impressive Rebel defense work had withstood bombardment and siege. It seemed that only a direct assault would bring down the defiant garrison.

Drawn up for battle, their division commander, Maj. Gen. George Strong, extolled, "Don't fire a musket on the way up, but go in and bayonet them at their guns." Then the general pointed at the 54th's 22-year-old color sergeant, John Wall, a student who had left school in Oberlin, Ohio, to join the unit. Strong challenged, "If this man should fall, who will lift the flag and carry on?" Robert Gould Shaw, the regiment's youthful colonel, did not hesitate to reply, "I will!" With that Shaw stepped forward and proclaimed, "I will go in advance with the National flag … We shall take the fort or die there! Good-bye!"

With these words, the brave Massachusetts infantrymen launched their attack with unloaded .577 Enfield rifles and cold steel, just as Strong had urged. Proceeding against a wall of Confederate fire, the attackers pressed forward. Casualties mounted, but onward they came. With tremendous courage some of the survivors finally "gained the parapet" where, according to a letter from Cpl. James Henry Gooding of the 54th, the colonel "seized the staff when the standard bearer fell, and in less than a minute" Shaw himself toppled as well.

At that Gooding reported, "When the men saw their gallant leader fall, they made a desperate effort to get him, but they were either shot down, or reeled in the ditch below. One man succeeded in getting hold of the State color staff, but the color was completely torn to pieces."

A formerly enslaved Virginian, Sgt. William Henry Carney, one of the few members of the unit who was not free-born, resolutely picked up the national colors, and although wounded four times, brought them back to safety, thereby saving them from capture. This act would later be recognized with the Medal of Honor.

The regimental sergeant-major, Lewis Douglass who was a son of the famed abolitionist Frederick Douglass, painted a vivid portrait of the intense fighting. "The enemy could be distinguished from our own men only by the light of bursting shell and the flash of the howitzer and musket. The darkness was so intense; the roar of artillery was so loud; the flight of grape and canister shot so rapid and destructive that it was absolutely impossible to preserve order."

The 54th's valiant efforts had not brought down Fort Wagner, but one thing was certain: no one could question whether the black man would fight. He had and would continue to do so throughout the war.

I: AFTERMATH OF BATTLE

A grisly duty: a soldier with a spade, wearing a poncho made of painted canvas or unbleached muslin covered with vulcanized Indian rubber as protection against the rain (sometimes dubbed "gum blankets" by the men) digs a hole to bury amputated arms and legs. In the background the wounded and dying are being treated at a field hospital consisting of little more than a few planks atop a table, a common scene as 285,245 Union soldiers, mostly infantrymen, were wounded during the course of the conflict.

Comrades, or in some instances local civilians, used stretchers, blankets, or whatever means possible to transport the wounded. Less fortunate individuals might have to make their own way without aid to medical assistance.

An injured man could remain on the field for long periods before being found. Many died as a result of exposure, loss of blood, or shock, before they could receive treatment. The Army of the Potomac's medical director, Surgeon Jonathan Letterman, would inaugurate a more systematic means of moving the victims of shot and shell via the establishment of an ambulance service in hopes of saving patients.

Not only were the soldiers at risk; the doctors could also fall prey to the enemy. For instance, at Antietam Dr Letterman reported that "some medical officers lost their lives in their devotion to duty", while "others sickened from excessive labor which they conscientiously and skillfully performed."

J: MUSICIANS

At the outbreak of the war few bands existed. Within a few months, however, Congress authorized regimental bands for all Regular Army infantry regiments. General Orders No. 38, published by the War Department on July 31 1861, specified that each infantry regiment, regular or volunteer, was entitled to two musicians per company along with one drum major and two principal musicians. Some of these musicians served with companies as field music, while others formed a regimental band, whose members were to be paid based on a special scale ranging from $17.50 per month for second-class musicians (their rank not necessarily their level of talent), to $105.50 per month for a drum major. By January 31 1862 bands had become so popular that a study was conducted to determine the costs of maintaining these martial musicians. When it was discovered that an infantry regimental band required over $13,000 in annual support, the secretary of war asked for their elimination from volunteer units.

During the summer of 1862 Congress agreed and required all volunteer bandsmen to be released from duty within 30 days. The abolition of bands did not mean they disappeared. In fact, they remained an integral part of the service, but at brigade level. At least 60 such organizations came into being, with the number of members set at 16 by Public Law 165 of July 17 1862. The same legislation reduced the pay scale.

Despite some high level opposition, bands were appreciated by officers and men alike. One soldier with the 24th Massachusetts Volunteer Infantry spoke of this positive attitude when he wrote about the regimental band under Patrick S. Gilmore. In his correspondence he indicated the musicians gave "splendid concerts, playing selections from the opera and some very pretty marches, quicksteps, waltzes, and the like, most of which are composed by himself [Gilmore] or by Ferdinand Zohler, a member of the band."

Nor did bands just perform in camp. In many instances they accompanied the troops into battle. For example, at Chancellorsville several Union bands held their ground near the front. When ordered to play the rousing patriotic tune "Rally Round the Flag" by their commander Gen. Winfield Scott Hancock, they did so despite the fact that shells were falling all around them.

Bands often received ornate or even fanciful uniforms, but in many instances they wore an outfit much like other enlisted men, such as the Regular Army infantry 1858-pattern dark blue wool nine-button frock coat, with the addition of sky-blue worsted lace trim on the chest. The sky-blue kersey trousers and forage cap with sloping visor (known as the "McDowell" pattern after Maj. Gen. Irvin McDowell, who for a brief time commanded the Army of the Potomac, and who favored this style of headgear) were also relatively common. Typically drums were painted blue with an eagle motif similar to regimental standards.

INDEX

Figures in **bold** refer to illustrations